EAR~~THSHINE~~

Gifts of Reflected Light

Bunny McBride

Wisbee Creek Press

Bath, Maine

FOR JAPHET

In everyone's life, at some time,
Our inner fire goes out . . .
And is then burst into flame by an encounter
With another human being.

~ Albert Schweitzer

CONTENTS

ACKNOWLEDGMENTS

During the long journey of writing this short book, two people paused with me numerous times to review multiple drafts of each essay – my husband Harald Prins and my sister Susan "Lily" Els. Their enduring interest, thoughtful insights and lively encouragement carried me over streams of doubt every time I questioned whether I was doing justice to the people and themes I felt impelled to write about. My gratitude for their help with this (and so much more in life) is immeasurable. Thanks, too, to the handful of friends who read or listened to the manuscript and offered comments that kept my inkwell full: Todd Hoffman, Kelly Jensen, Martha Moyer, Lisa Redfern, Lark Rodman and Alejandro Torres. Most of all, my thanksgiving goes to the people profiled on these pages, which are, essentially, love letters to them.

Bunny McBride, Bath, Maine, November 2023

INTRODUCTION – REFLECTION

You are a wellspring in my desert,
a moonbeam in my night. ~ Anon

The moon always has another story to tell. After all, it rises and sets daily, and never in exactly the same phase and circumstance. That's true for us humans, too. And like the moon, we shine more brightly in some situations than in others. Sometimes, we have barely a sliver of glimmer to give. Other times we're in full-blown glow and brighten every encounter. There are also instances when, like a new moon, it seems we have little beyond darkness to express. During those moments, it's wondrous to suddenly notice someone else's light illuminating our being. The transformative impact is similar to that of *earthshine*, which occurs when the dark part of the moon is softly lit by sunlight reflecting off the Earth. I've had that experience quite often – the feeling of being touched and shined up by the light of others. *Humanshine.* I've noticed that if I embrace that gift of light and fuel it with gratitude, it reflects onto someone else and from them onto another and then another… It's all reflected light, echoing out from an original source.

For earthshine, that primal source is the sun. For humans, it's a divine energy variously referred to as God, Spirit, Truth, Love, Infinite Mind, Divine Energy, the Universal Life Force and a host of other names.

In contrast to stars, lightning and bioluminescent organisms such as fireflies, glowworms and jellyfish, the light humans emanate cannot be measured in wavelengths or frequencies. It is a kind of spiritual luminescence revealed in certain ways of being that inspire, comfort and teach us – and sometimes alter the way we look at the world and our place in it.

These days, I find myself thinking often about individuals who have cast light in my direction during the many decades of my lifetime. Holding them in memory's hand like a bundle of moonbeams, I've been pulling them out, one at a time, considering their particular qualities and recalling our shared experiences. The result is the book in hand, a collection of contemplative stories about people whose lives have given me pause and prompted me to reflect upon choices, priorities and what each of us brings to the feast of Life.

Part profile, part parable, some of these stories were originally conceived for my book, *By the Light of the Moon: Reflections on Wholeness of Being*. They didn't quite fit there, but I still yearned to write them, along with several others about people who have been occupying my thoughts and filling me with grateful contemplation during this autumn season of life. Each and every person sketched on these pages has enlightened me on what it means to live bravely, engagingly, purposefully, resiliently, joyfully, generously. They come from different parts of the globe and varied walks of life – from poet, author and dancer to cellist, clairvoyant and teacher, from soldier, spiritual guide and activist to anthropologist, basketmaker and fetus. Some were steady companions over many years. Others I spent relatively little time with. One I never met in person.

Often, when I first meet someone – while hiking a trail, riding a train, chatting in a grocery checkout line – I have a sense that they have something important to tell me, a feeling that there's some kind of underlying relationship, which, given time, could be realized in a meaningful way. Occasionally, the connection is so strong and close to the surface, that we fall into it easily. Even if it's for just a moment, it conveys a burst of delight or even insight. Other times, it's deeply hidden and would likely require serious excavation to unearth. And then there are those exceptional occasions that leave me with the impression that an encounter was orchestrated for a profound purpose by some power beyond me. That's true with everyone portrayed in this

3

book, from Steven, a poet I happened upon in a bookstore, to Sarah, a Mi'kmaq basketmaker I met while working on a Native rights case in Maine.

I could have written many more stories than the dozen included here. I could have described the sweet influence of one person's boundless faith and forgiveness, the revitalizing effect of a music career focused on comfort and healing, the awakening born of witnessing a friend transform tragedy into strength and conviction, or how the heart opens when you see someone devote a lifetime to helping others find the full measure of their being. . . The list goes on. But this is what I have for now – twelve stories about people whose lives have touched mine and changed me for the better.

WHEN LIFE TOSSES YOU UP

Dignity is like air. When you breathe easily,
you don't think about it.
But when you don't have enough of it,
all you can think about is air, air, more air.

~ Aigul Aubanova

It was her hair that brought us together. This is how it happened: I was directing a community center for low-income minority kids in Boston. Henrietta made a donation. I wrote a thank-you note. Then she called to thank me for my thank-you. As we talked, she asked if I knew someone who might be willing to come to her apartment to cut and color her hair since it was difficult for her to get to a salon and maneuver herself into specialized beautician chairs. I told her I could do it, never imagining that opening a bottle of hair dye in her presence would transform the way I looked at the world and my place in it.

Henrietta's apartment was a tiny place brimming with big ideas – floor-to-ceiling bookshelves and a wide array of visitors drawn to the deep, life-altering conversations that happened in her company. Her questions were penetrating, her insights profound. She always wanted to hear the long version of any story that had meaning, and she never took her eyes off you when you spoke. She knew about listening – the essence of empathy. Although she usually listened more than she talked, surely that was not because she believed other lives were more compelling than her remarkable journey. Rather, she understood that each life she came to know expanded and enriched her own sense of being.

The day she came into the world in 1909, her parents named her Henrietta Delancey Henkle. That last name was no match for the bold contemplative historical novels that would become her hallmark – books about the Underground Railroad, the Holocaust, the United Nations, Shakespeare, the Apostle Paul, and women who shaped history. . . So, after reaching adulthood, she changed Henkle to Buckmaster – her maternal grandmother's maiden name. It had an intellectual air, a seeker's promise, an activist's kick.

Henrietta grew up in New York City. Her father was a newspaper editor, her mother a housewife. Surrounded by books, she learned to read and write before starting kindergarten at the Friends Seminary. Her educated, middle-class parents adored their bright and beautiful daughter and afforded her every opportunity. Life looked nothing but promising.

Then everything changed. At age seven, Henrietta contracted polio at the tail end of an epidemic that struck some 8000 New York City children, 2000 of whom died. She survived, but thereafter, depended upon a wheelchair or heavy metal braces that cut into her legs while making it possible for her to hobble short distances ever so slowly. Her parents did all they could to shelter her from discomfort and loss. They minimized activities that focused attention on her physical limitations, and when she reached adolescence, they encouraged her keen intellectual capacities by enrolling her in Brearley – a private, rigorous, all-girl's school.

As a 12-year-old Henrietta wrote her first published piece – a story for *Child Life* magazine. By the time she graduated from high school in 1927, she had penned several reviews for *The New York Times Book Review*. Certain that she wanted to be an author and eager to widen her world toward that end, she decided to forego college and "go to Europe instead."

Henrietta read voraciously, and every page she turned fueled her determination to succeed as a writer. Her first novel came off the press in 1934, her second two years later. Between the publication dates of those books, she lost her father, who she described as "the one person who always made me feel secure and amplified." But there was solace. Within that same timeframe, she also found the love of her life, a man who seemed ready to partner her in all the ways she'd dreamed of. Peter Stephens was a kindred spirit, an aspiring British playwright three years her junior. They met in church. Captivated by her intelligence and luminous, deep-set eyes, he invited her to a movie. They drove to the theater, but after the show, he suggested they walk the eight blocks home because the night was so lovely. Since polio struck, she had never walked that far. But now, exhilarated by his innocent sense of her capability, as well as by his compassionate pauses, she covered the distance. By the time they reached her Greenwich Village apartment, she had fallen in love.

In 1936, they married and began figuring out how to do life together as two artful bohemians, one of whom had special physical needs. Although Peter always encouraged Henrietta to walk, often when they were out and about, he pushed her along in her wheelchair. On nights when she felt especially weary and removed her braces right after dinner, he carried her from the couch to their bed. But, in other ways she carried him. He earned a modest income writing articles for the British Information Services New York office, but he yearned to make his living penning plays and poems. In this, his wife served as muse, mentor, booster and frequent coauthor. As for her own work, she always had a new book project underway and garnered income through royalties and freelance work for numerous newspapers and magazines. She and Peter were enthusiastic about each other's creative endeavors, talking endlessly about them and offering keen critical feedback.

Henrietta's ambition to do something meaningful with her life was enormous – perhaps to counter what she referred to as "the world's appraisal of me as a cripple." Asked if she would have been the same person without polio," she answered, "How do I know? What I do know is that when life has tossed you up, you are not complacent. You are impelled to find meaning and purpose and to develop *character*." She found all of these through work, social action and especially through deep metaphysical exploration focused on transcending physical limitations and transforming social inequities through broadcasting knowledge, insights and love. She succeeded in rising above the physical restrictions of polio to the point that it never kept her from having an engaged and fulfilling life. But she wanted more. She held to the idea that metaphysics could do for her what doctors could not – make her legs function normally.

In 1941, Harper Collins published Henrietta's historical novel, *Let My People Go,* lauded by critics and endorsed by Richard Wright as "a book of major importance, [remarkable for its] depth, width and compassion." Elsewhere, Wright described it as "an impassioned and provocative depiction of the revolutionary impulses of a nation." The book brought her fame, bolstered her confidence, and sharpened her sense of purpose. She spent three years researching and writing this poignant portrayal of the anti-slavery movement, and she became deeply committed to what she learned through the endeavor. During that time, she told her diary: "I take on myself like stigmata all the cruelties of persecution and hatred. To me, the only real beauty is in the fostering of each person's dignity, and everything else must be subservient to that."

In the course of her lifetime, Henrietta authored more than two dozen books. On her pages and in person, she became known for her wide humanitarian interests, which included spirited participation in the Civil Rights Movement and social action groups fighting for the rights of laborers, refugees, women, prisoners and Native Americans – not to mention animals. She felt a kinship with all life and shaped her personal and professional priorities accordingly.

Often called upon to give public lectures, Henrietta once commented, "I spoke for anyone who asked me within the field of minority rights. My question was always, 'You're for the rights of minorities? Okay.

What time do you want me?' I spoke for groups left, right and center."

She also wrote for minority publications, such as *The Negro Quarterly*, and joined or donated to numerous organizations committed to the disenfranchised and downtrodden at home and abroad. These included progressive organizations such as the Artists Front to Win the War, the Committee for Equal Justice, and the National Council of Arts, Sciences, and Professions, plus various groups pressing for decolonization around the world. She gave little thought to rumors that many of the organizations she spoke for, wrote for, or contributed to were being surveilled by the U.S. Federal Bureau of Investigation as possible communist fronts.

At the end of World War 2, the deadliest conflict in human history, Henrietta joined the Congress of American Women. The organization selected her and 12 other members as delegates for the 1945 World Peace Conference in France, sponsored by the Women's International Democratic Federation. Eight hundred women from thirty-two countries attended the gathering to consider post-war problems. These included food and housing shortages, orphaned children, rehabilitation of the wounded, restoration of democracy and international relations, as well as the status of women. Henrietta wrote about it for *Women's Day* magazine. A few years later, she penned, *Bread from Heaven,* an historical novel about a young man and a maimed child in his care – concentration camp survivors striving to find their place in a small and unwelcoming American town. *The New York Times* compared it to Alan Paton's internationally acclaimed *Cry the Beloved Country,* noting that it embodied "the same search for a more merciful understanding of men, the same belief that wherever there is intolerance and stupidity there is also altruism and courage…"

When I first met Henrietta, she was 65 and I was 24. By then, she had faced many challenges beyond polio – none greater than Peter leaving her for a walking woman after 15 years of marriage. She had recently become editor of the art and literary pages of an international newspaper, *The Christian Science Monitor*, and she was in the throes of turning that section on its ear. She sought out writers of conscience and transformed the pages into an inter-ethnic, inter-class dialog. It became one of the most respected and thought-provoking sections of the paper – a place where artists, poets, prisoners and a wide range of movers and shakers had a voice. Some of the best-known thinkers in the world appeared on her pages, but she also nurtured young, unknown writers who yearned to make a difference – writers like me.

In the early days of our friendship, I took a writing workshop with an old Australian essayist, who wrote often for Henrietta's section of the paper. At his urging, I began submitting my essays and poems – and somewhat to my amazement, she published them. In the years that followed, I spent increasingly more time writing, sometimes from faraway places in Africa, China, the Arctic. I began penning news features for various publications, while continuing to write essays, which most often found a home on Henrietta's pages.

By 1978, Henrietta and I had become close friends, and I signed on to be her assistant editor for a year. She talked me into the job, saying I'd be doing her a favor. But I soon came to understand that she did it to mentor me. She encouraged me to weave substantive information into my contemplative essays – to keep both facts and feelings in sight, as if looking at the rabbit/duck visual pun and managing to see both at once. She helped hone my editing skills, demanding a light but effective touch that stays true to the voice of each writer while bringing into sharper focus any examples of, or insights on, human dignity – which she saw as a vital element in all forms of writing. She imparted the importance of dignity toward all life – placing gourmet cheese in the Havahart mousetrap she kept under her desk and insisting that we reuse every manilla envelope that came into the office, because, after all, trees paid for our mail with their lives.

When my year of working with Henrietta ended, I left Boston for New York to get a master's degree in anthropology, which led to Native rights work in Maine. Time with Henrietta diminished, but we never lost touch. We wrote to one another, I visited her frequently in Boston, and after I moved to Maine a mutual friend drove her up for a long-planned visit away from the city. That was the last time we were together face to face.

After a decade of friendship, I knew Henrietta well. But in the wake of her death in 1983, I discovered how much I did not know. She left me her personal papers – diaries, newsclips, magazine articles, research files and photographs. Whenever I dig into her boxes, I find words and images by her, of her and about her that speak to me and deepen our friendship even though she's no longer present in the old way.

Among her papers I came upon a large photograph of Ruth St. Denis, the iconic "mother of modern dance." I wondered why it was there and how she came to have it. The answer came in the early 1990s, when I was researching the life story of the Penobscot Indian dancer Molly Spotted Elk (1903-77). I read widely about other famous dancers of her era, especially those with whom she had shared a stage, including St.

14

Denis. To my astonishment, in reading St. Denis' autobiography, I learned that Henrietta had been her ghost writer. This hit me as a heart-rending surprise: First, because of the realization that my dear empathetic friend, who could barely walk with braces, had managed to inhabit and relay in convincing first-person prose the story of a woman who moved with remarkable freedom and grace on stages all around the world. And second, because I had failed to ask the question that would have prompted Henrietta to tell me about this. For me, this was an unforgettable lesson that the quest of coming to know and understand one another is never finished. We must make a point of asking, even when we think we know. Ideally, while they're still here.

Among Henrietta's papers, I also came across the 30-page 1956 testimony she presented to the U.S. House Un-American Activities Committee in response to accusations that she affiliated with organizations and publications that the government labeled as subversive or communist fronts – the Civil Rights Congress, the Congress of American Women, Contemporary Writers, *New Masses* and *The Negro Quarterly*, among others. In her statement, she summarized her involvement with such groups: "The basis for my activities has always been humane, never political. . ." After expounding on that, she offered a writer's perspective on her choices: "I think a writer stands very close to life, and that her identification with men and women of all races, classes and creeds is indissoluble. The world is hers to see as clearly as possible. She cuts off her own hand if she separates herself from any other human being in joy or in sorrow, in conflict or in success."

Henrietta's 1956 testimony was a kind of autobiography of values, tracking the ethics that undergirded her writing. It included the story of New York based federal investigators showing up at her home three years earlier and interrogating her for several hours in an effort to unearth communist connections with various foundations, including the Guggenheim, which had awarded her a fellowship in 1944. Their questions, she wrote, "were almost entirely designed to solicit names. . . . I declined firmly, well aware that I was in my plight because individuals had speculated about me. . . . I was told I would be subpoenaed to appear in Washington, and that five trusted government informants would connect me with the Communist Party. I replied that I could easily prove that the five informants were five perjurers."

In her testimony, Henrietta also told what happened after her husband left her in 1949. To cover the bills in her new one-income household, she took a part-time editing job at *Women's Day*. Soon thereafter, the magazine ran a one-page "inspirational" piece by her. "Unfortunately," she said, "my article – or rather my name – brought down the heavens." Using her to make a point, the reactionary newspaper, *The Tablet*, called for a nationwide boycott of A & P grocery stores, a major distributor of the magazine's 3.3 million weekly copies, on the ground that *Women's Day* employed editors and writers affiliated with Communist front organizations, such as the Congress of American Women. As Henrietta told it, "A & P was involved in a government anti-trust suit and apparently felt that it had enough on its hands without me to complicate matters. I was fired overnight with no severance pay, and I was not eligible for unemployment insurance. My financial plight has been disastrous ever since, because I appear to be on a number of blacklists."

Ultimately, Henrietta's testimony earned her a "not guilty" verdict, but the accusations she faced caused long-term hardship. She continued writing and scraped by on book royalties, but it wasn't until the *Monitor* hired her as an editor in the early 1970s that she re-found what felt like true professional and economic equilibrium.

One Saturday morning in 1978, I received an unusual call from Henrietta. Her erudite voice sounded uncharacteristically shaky. "Can you come over?" she implored. "I keep having the same dream. I need to tell someone." I grabbed my coat and made the 15-minute walk to her apartment. I found her sitting on her big bed, propped up against pillows, with a crumpled tissue in one hand. I sat down next to her and took her empty hand in mine. "Tell me about your dream."

"I'm outside on a beautiful grassy hillside. There are wildflowers. The sky is blue. The slope is steep. I'm running uphill – *running!* The wind is lifting my hair and I'm laughing." She paused. Her eyes welled. "It's a wonderful dream. The problem is, I don't know if it's a promise or if it's an omen of what will never be." I longed to assure her that it was a promise, but those words didn't come. Instead, we just sat together in silence. After some time, I said what I felt certain was true: "It's not an omen."

Five years later, after I'd left Boston, finished graduate school and settled in Maine, I received a call from a mutual friend telling me Henrietta had passed away and asking me to come down to help sort through her things. I hung up the phone and closed my eyes in shock and sorrow. Gripped by loss, I couldn't move from my chair. Then, suddenly, a vivid image appeared in my mind, like the opening of a film starring Henrietta: There she was, running uphill under a blue sky, laughing, the wind lifting her hair. . .

And here I am, many years after that reverie, sitting at my desk, feeling her companionship as I so often do when writing. Tacked to my computer on a well-worn piece of paper are her words, reminding me that a writer "cuts off her own hand if she separates herself from any other human being in joy or in sorrow."

THE SOUND OF ANTS WALKING

Instructions for life: Pay attention. Be astonished.
Tell about it. ~ Mary Oliver

In broad daylight, and at noon,
Yesterday I saw the moon. ~ Longfellow

I was camped out on the floor in the history corner of Brentano's bookstore in Boston, immersed in taking notes from several books about West Africa.

"Can I help you?"

The voice was unusual. Like molasses with edges. Glancing up, I saw blue jeans, a collared sweater, wavy brown hair and dark, slightly slanted eyes that narrowed to bright slits as the bookseller smiled, awaiting my response.

"I'm all set," I said, pleased to be surrounded by books that made me feel I was already on the trip I was planning. Engaged and content, I didn't imagine that someone might make me feel even more so. I turned my attention back to the books at hand.

Undeterred, he crouched down beside me, glanced at my biblio piles, and asked, "What are you working on?"

And so began the first of countless conversations with Steven, a poet determined to turn his craft into a livelihood. As our friendship grew, I watched him do that. I became accustomed to having him arrive at my door saying, "I can't talk. I need a pen. A poem's coming!" Every time we visited, he had something to share with me – a stanza, a single evocative word, a new poetry book he'd added to his collection. He encouraged me to come to open mic poetry readings at Stone Soup café, where words were the primary sustenance. In the course of time, his poems appeared in numerous literary journals and anthologies. He also authored several chapbooks and gathered into one book a collection of his conversations with some of the craft's most beloved and influential voices, including William Stafford, Mary Oliver, and Seamus Heaney. He titled it "Giving Their Word," suggesting that poetry is a promise to be true to oneself and others. In the best of times, he compounded my own energy and light. And during the doldrums his creative spirit reignited mine.

One of Steven's greatest joys is bringing poetry to people not inclined to attend a reading or browse the poetry aisle in a bookstore. He's a master in generating delight by injecting poems into communities in unexpected ways, such as his "Poet-Tree" project, which involved gathering verses from local poets and displaying them on laminated cards hanging from trees throughout his town. And his "Red Letter Poems" project – conceived as a one-off mailing of poems in hand-addressed red envelopes to 1000 randomly-selected households – ultimately went online, with a new poem going out every Friday to thousands within and beyond the United States. Each delivery, said Steven, was intended to be "a little Sabbath candle after a stressful week." Something to brighten dull or dark moods.

In addition to disseminating poetry on screens, paper and cards dangling from trees, Steven spreads its magic through public readings and teaching – as a poet-in-residence at various schools and as Poet Laureate for Arlington, Massachusetts. I'm just one of many to be swept up in his theatrical readings and fervent narratives about poetry's fascinating forms, from sonnet to villanelle.

Perhaps more than anything, time with Steven taught me how a poet's perspective awakens the senses. That was especially true one lazy weekend day when he and I lay on our backs in the grassy park near Harvard University's Weld Boathouse on the north bank of the Charles River. It was Saturday afternoon on a spring day that teased anyone who stayed inside. Eyes skyward, we saw a nearly full moon returning our gaze. I love it when the moon shows herself in the daytime. As often as that happens, I'm still surprised when she catches my attention during those hours when the sun rules the sky.

"Can you see the Man in the Moon?" I asked, even though the lunar markings were at that moment too faint to reveal his face clearly.

"No, but I see the Rabbit," said Steven, sounding pleased with himself and slightly sly.

"Rabbit?" I asked, lifting a skeptical eyebrow.

"Your name is Bunny, and you don't know about the Rabbit in the Moon?"

I laughed, quite certain he was pulling my leg. But, as it turns out, the Man in Moon really does have a neighbor. The Man and the Rabbit are both examples of visual pareidolia – the phenomenon of seeing faces, figures, or forms in the patterns of clouds, smoke, shadows, wood grain, and so forth. The moon's geography, characterized by light-hued highlands and dark lava "seas" visible to the naked eye from Earth, presents an array of markings that people in many cultures have perceived as the image of a rabbit. Legend has it that the moon is also host to a beetle, a toad, a dragon slayer, and a lady reading a book.

Stories about the Moon Rabbit are especially common in East Asian folklore but can also be found in the Americas. Cree Indians tell of a rabbit that yearned to ride the moon and talked a crane into taking him there. All the way up Rabbit clutched the bird's ankles with all his might, chafing his paws and stretching Crane's legs. When they reached the moon, Rabbit touched Crane's brow with a bleeding foot. That, say the Cree, is why cranes have long legs and red caps. According to the tale, Rabbit still rides the moon to this day, so when the light is right, we can see him from Earth.

Although I couldn't make ear nor tail of Moon Rabbit that afternoon, I wanted to hear more about it, but Steven was taking our conversation in a different direction. "There's a lot to *see* from this vantage point, but even more to *hear*," he said, using his dramatic poetry recitation voice. "We humans are so sight-centric that we miss most of what life is telling us through our other senses. When we understand something, we say, 'I *see*,' rather than, "Ahhhh, I *smell*.'"

"How short-sighted of us," I said, reinforcing his point.

"It's a loss for everyone, but a crime for writers."

Then he offered me a challenge: "Close your eyes, pay close attention and count how many layers of sound you detect."

"Is there a goal?"

"Go for ten."

Lids lowered, I give myself over to my ears. The first thing I hear is people – laughing, calling to each other and their dogs. A dog barks – *yap yap yap*. Then another – a deep *woof woof*. Next, I notice traffic – trucks and cars on Memorial Drive. I'm sorry to realize that while out of sight from this park, the road is not out of ear shot. And now I notice the rumble of motorboats, which surprises me since Memorial Drive separates us from the river. I'm happy about the boat noise, thinking that if I listen hard enough, I might be able to hear the river. But what comes up next is another motor – a lawnmower somewhere to my right. I inhale and smell fresh cut grass. From another direction comes the sound of a bell – a faint but deeply resonant *bong!*, followed by three more of the same. I must have missed the clock tower's first chime because it's more likely five o'clock than four. When the bells stop, I detect a coxswain shouting through a megaphone to his crew of rowers. I strain my ears, reaching for the dip and splash of oars. I think I can just barely hear them – but suspect it's my imagination creating a sound to go with the coxswain's commands.

I mention the soundings to Steven as they come – naming each with one or two words in a quiet voice so as not to disturb our listening. After I say, "splashing oars?" he whispers, "Every sound you've mentioned – except the dogs – is human made. You'll never get to ants walking if you don't go deeper."

I try hard, practically inhaling through my ears. Suddenly, I'm aware of the wind – so soft, a barely decipherable breath skimming past my ears. I picture sailboats at a standstill. Bird sounds begin to register. Trillings and twitters, liquid and sweet. Caroling notes, rising and falling in pitch. Ducks. Warblers. Swallows. Robins. Pigeons. A flicker? A kingbird? Then come the insects – buzzing, whining, whirring, chirping, creaking. Next, to my delight, I hear wings flapping. Birds, not insects, although wouldn't it be amazing to hear the flutter of butterfly wings? I decide the birds must be small, because the flapping is fast. Pleased with this, I strain my ears for something more subtle. Recalling the Rabbit in the Moon, I'm wondering if there might be a real rabbit under one of the nearby bushes and whether it would be possible to hear it chewing. Nothing.

I turn my attention to ants. No matter how hard
I try, I can't hear them walking.

Biking back to my apartment at dusk, surrounded
by the cacophony of traffic, I caught glimpses of birds
flitting through the air and of the moon climbing up the
sky. But giving them my attention was risky on the busy
road, so I pedaled fast, aiming for the relative serenity of
my garden apartment in a brownstone on a side street.
Parking my bike, I heard the *cheer-up* song of sparrows.
I sighed, grateful for my postage-stamp yard and city
parks, vowing to spend more time in each. I thought
about the natural world living in the city – and
immediately noticed that I hadn't thought about the city
being held in the nature. I owed the second thought to
Steven's lesson on tuning in.

That afternoon has stayed with me for decades.
One of several momentous call-to-attention experiences
in my life, it taught me the importance of patient
alertness in the natural world – of watching and listening,
as well as sniffing, feeling and tasting for any subtle shift
that tells you something's about to appear or happen: the
temperature drop before a squall; the counter sway of a
lion's tail among tall grasses bending in a Serengeti
breeze; the mucky scent announcing that water released
from the Blue River dam has widened the lake's

mudflats; the honking of geese before their giant V formation passes overhead; the low growl of our dog just before a fox skirts the edge of our woodland shore; the kitten-soft touch of pussy willow buds telling you that springtime greenery is about to emerge...

Thanks to Steven, all of my ethnography students learned about listening for layers of sound and employing all the senses when researching and writing. I've even offered extra credit for exercising non-sight senses by going through an entire day blindfolded (guided by a friend) and then writing about the experience. One of the most effective assignments I've given them is to pen a scent memory after reading a narrative on smell in Diane Ackerman's enlivening book, *Natural History of the Senses*. Nothing, says Ackerman, is more evocative than smell: "Hit a tripwire of smell and memories explode all at once."

I've often wished I could ask dogs to report on their scent memories since their noses have some 200 million olfactory receptors compared to our five million. We humans may be disadvantaged in this category compared to canines, but most of us don't begin to tap into our full smell potential, nor that of all the other senses we possess. Equipped as we are with perception organs, it's clear we are meant to pay attention. We just need a little determination and practice.

The life of disability rights advocate Helen Keller (1880-1968) hints at our capacities. As recounted by Ackerman, although Keller was blind and deaf, her remaining senses became so finely attuned that she could write in lengthy detail about the "whelm of life's aromas, tastes, touches and feelings, which she explored with the voluptuousness of a courtesan." She could discern someone's line of work by the way that person smelled. And most remarkably, when placing her hands on a radio to enjoy music, she could distinguish the cornets from the strings.

I wonder if Keller, hands to the ground, could have felt the delicate vibrations of ants walking? Although, thanks to Steven's nudge, my own listening skills have expanded, I've yet to hear those tiny beings on the move through either my ears or my hands. However, countless times, when the sun has slipped away and a full moon owns the night sky, I have seen the Moon Rabbit. Striving to listen has helped me to see. And, ironically, when I listen for what Moon Rabbit has to say, I detect something exceedingly rare and exquisite: the brilliant sound of silence.

BECAUSE WE ARE

If you knew what I know about the power of giving,
you would not let a single meal pass without
sharing it in some way. ~ Buddha

It happened four decades ago in the tiny village of
Faoune in southern Senegal. I went there with a friend
who published a self-help development magazine for
rural communities in West Africa. He was traveling the
region to talk with locals about the journal's impact on
their daily lives. In Faoune, we were hosted by a man
named Demba, a community organizer who lived there
and worked with young farmers to help them diversify
and increase their crop yields and income streams.

Demba was a stocky fellow with a captivating
big-toothed smile and skin the warm brown hue of
tamarind nuts. He exuded an aura of being everyone's
big brother. Day after day during our stay, I watched a
steady stream of villagers come to him for advice,
conversation, stories, or a good laugh. I found myself
doing the same. On my last night there, after we and
several others finished eating a dinner of spicy
vegetables and rice from a shared bowl beneath an open

sky, Demba and I took one last walk together. An ample moon lit our way as we sauntered along the sandy trail that meandered around peanut fields, vegetable gardens and mud houses. It was one of those enchanted nights with stars blinking from horizon to horizon and a gentle breeze whispering through the scene. The sort of night that prompts big questions.

I mused aloud, "Demba, do you ever ask yourself, "Who am I?""?

It took him a moment to respond, "I've never thought of that question."

This was not in the realm of answers I might have expected. It seemed far-fetched that Demba had never considered a question that occupied just about all the young people I knew back home in the States, myself included. During that year in particular, I'd thought about it a lot – reaching for renewed self-awareness, independence and peace of mind as my first marriage was falling apart. Demba's response seemed almost like an affront to that effort. We walked in silence for a minute or two. He did not rush in to fill the pause.

"But the search for oneself, doesn't that interest you?" I ventured.

"It's not something I've given thought to. Tell me about it."

Still disbelieving, I tried to explain. "Well, where I come from, most people in our generation think that figuring out who they are is the most important of all quests. It's usually done solo – in a quiet corner at home, or outside on a walk, atop a mountain or staring up at the moon and stars on a night like this. Whatever the setting, you slip away on your own and try to discern just exactly who you are – what makes you unique and therefore significant in this world. During these private inquiries you might seek answers by reading about other people's self-searches, or you might totally turn your thought inward and fully contemplate the subject of 'I,' asking, *What do I value? What do I have to offer? How do I know if I'm being honest with myself? Am I on the right path? Who am I?"*

"Well," Demba shrugged, "I've never asked, 'Who am I?' But I often ask, 'What is the purpose of life? It's similar to your question, but it includes the context of the individual – the community in which one lives. The answer to this question is not in books or in being alone, but in being with others and in giving to one another."

Once again, our conversation paused. The night was so still that I could hear both of us breathing as we walked. I considered the words and the life of this man who grew up on a continent where familial obligation was a powerful and far-reaching social force. As soon as he became a working adult with an income, he was expected to share his earnings with anyone in his extended family who came to him for help. In the short time I'd been in Faoune, I'd already witnessed him reach into his pocket for others who weren't even members of his family. I wondered how he felt about that and if he could ever realize his full potential while wrapped in a wide web of collective expectations and responsibilities.

"Do you ever resent it when others ask you for money? Do you ever feel held back by them?"

His answer was a slow, thoughtful *No...*, followed by this: "How can I be happy if my brother is sad? I have a responsibility to my family – not only because of social pressure, but because I've chosen to be committed. I don't feel held back by them. A person can climb to the top of a mountain more quickly alone than with a group, but it would be pointless to arrive at the top and have no one there to share the view."

I was in my twenties when I took this walk with Demba and I made notes about our conversation in my journal. At the time, I drank in his words as if they spoke for a continent of people – with the exception of criminals, corrupt leaders and warlords, of course. Later, I came to realize that his devotion to living life for the whole of his family – actually, for his entire community

– was well beyond the fundamental norm of obligatory sharing with kin that I'd witnessed repeatedly across Africa. That basic norm was a kind of mutual social security manifested in reciprocity, whereas Demba's outreach sprang from his distinctly generous heart and a solid conviction that doing unto others as you would have them do unto you is the only way to live a meaningful life.

Everything about Demba communicated commitment to the idea that, ultimately, one person's suffering diminishes the life experience of all of us. A decade earlier, he had left a well-paid position at an accounting firm in the capital city of Dakar and moved 200 miles south to Faoune. He had a vision of helping young farmers think beyond focusing on boom-bust cash crops like peanuts, which depleted the soil and were subject to the wiles of government pricing. His goal was to encourage mixed farming that included food cultivation, fueled local markets, increased family incomes and helped end hunger. He set his sights on building a rural movement based on community self-determination and sustainability. Eventually, he gained the trust of farmers and together they established an agricultural organization that loosened the grip of poverty and hunger, as well as illiteracy and cultural loss, within and beyond Faoune.

Although the breadth and depth of Demba's community spirit surpassed that of most, it nonetheless sprang from what I think of as a core human ethic – an inherent inkling that something is amiss when the welfare of an individual far exceeds or falls far below that of others in their community. I saw this evidenced in countless ways during years of work travel in various African countries. I saw the sick, the elderly, the orphan, the disabled, all sustained within the family circle rather than in institutions. In Gambia, I met a blind man whose grandchildren took turns guiding him. Every afternoon he could be found walking around town holding one end of a long stick atop his shoulder, the other end propped on the shoulder of a grandchild in front of him. By helping him to navigate, they lightened the load of his dark world.

The idea that an individual's problem belongs to the community can also be seen in the way many traditional healers treat a sick patient: Believing that illness never happens in isolation, they treat the entire family and sometimes the community as well.

During a severe drought in Mali, I watched three tiny children sitting around a bowl of porridge with one spoon, each taking a mouthful and then passing the spoon on to the next, as if that were the only way to behave. About that drought it was said that the only thing more remarkable than its cruelty was the fact that so many survived on so little because of the powerful ethic of sharing.

This carries over to many Africans living abroad. In the States, I've noticed that, almost invariably, no matter how meager their earnings, they – like other immigrants from developing countries – send money back to their families, limiting their own comfort and consumption to do so.

So there it is: the philosophy of shared wellbeing and reciprocity that undergirds an age-old, life-sustaining social ethic. It's reflected in a proverb found in numerous languages across Africa: *I am because we are.* I mentioned this maxim to Demba during our walk and asked him what he thought it meant. "It means we're all interconnected," he said. I remained quiet, waiting for more. He continued, "The realization of each person's potential is important, but the question is how someone's success helps improve the community around them. It's our interconnectedness that makes us human, so there is no point in considering your life or your accomplishments in isolation."

Alongside the notes I made in my journal about what Demba said during our moonlit walk, I wrote down my own simple summary of his lesson: "Life is for discovering your part in the whole of being. What you do affects everyone and everything. It had better be good."

BEFORE DISCARDING

Life is a balance of holding on and letting go ~ Rumi

We had traveled hundreds of slow sweltering miles on the mighty Niger River to the place where it skirts the edge of the Sahara Desert in the West African country of Mali. Stepping ashore gingerly from a leaky wooden pirogue, we followed a sandy track toward the bush taxi that would carry us the final five miles to our destination: the ancient city of Timbuktu.

During its golden age from the 14th-16th centuries, Timbuktu was the southern gateway to trans-Saharan trade. It was a magnificent intellectual, spiritual and commercial hub, renowned for its libraries, grand mosques and an endless stream of camel caravans laden with salt, gold and other prized commodities. As we approached from a distance, it rose up like a majestic mirage enthroned upon the horizon. Its mud-and timber structures had a beauty not of color, but of silhouette and line. However, once we were within its walls, Timbuktu seemed less like a desert queen of fortune and more like a sovereign without a kingdom. I was dismayed by obvious widespread poverty and disappointed by decrepit buildings worn, cracked and crumbled by relentless sun and seasonal storms.

As our weeks in Timbuktu and other desert settlements continued, as we endured with their inhabitants under the flattening weight of the sun, my impression shifted again. I began to marvel at the unlikely raising of a city or town in a sea of scorching sands. There is a distinct integrity to the buildings: The walls are made of the very earth on which they stand, and the roofs are constructed out of local palm-tree joists crossed with branches and covered with palm-frond matting and fine mud. Moreover, they hold a depth of history that reaches back more than a millennium: Dozens of generations have worked, rested and worshipped within these walls; centuries of blazing sun, pounding winter rains and blinding spring sandstorms have textured the surface of every edifice and tested the fortitude of every person.

Perhaps it is because of the enormous effort and almost pitiful patience required to build and survive here, that given a thoughtful gaze, these places exude a subtle and sublime kind of beauty. The structures and those who abide with them stand as stoic monuments to a glorious past that insists there must be a future.

But what sort of future? Timbuktu's golden era has long passed. Its prominent position in trade has ended. Its climate is harsher than ever with frequent and severe droughts. Worse, its social fabric is ripped and frayed, with government corruption and recurring rebel uprisings holding hope and progress hostage. There is no shared vision on how to move forward.

Amid the distressing demise, architecture may offer a key. Like sandcastles on a beach, desert towns appear to be made of one piece, as if tugged up from the earth by some mighty magnet. And so it was with a man we met, named Moustapha. He, in contrast to the fragmentation all around him, appears to be made of one piece. From the moment we met, I was struck by his predisposition to turn problems into opportunities and by the way he blended past and present into a way of being that to me seemed exquisitely balanced and whole. With wonder and admiration, I observed how he selected roots from his traditional culture and branches from the modern world and wove them together with knowledge and forethought into a kind of wisdom for the ages. While some of his countrymen fight ferociously over resources and drop time-honored ways and insights to race empty-handed toward the materialism and technological innovations that Western society has dangled and thrust before them, Moustapha carries into each new day the deep history of his African people. During one visit, when I was gravely ill, he sang me poems of that history which, for him, remained alive, beating in the core of his being, participating in the shaping of his thoughts and desires. His music told me that without roots, branches die. It helped beckon me back to life.

Moustapha has to duck the doorways of this region's ancient buildings. At 6'5", he appears even taller, with a pointed black beard lengthening his angular ebony face and flowing white robes elongating his lanky body. "Tall enough to collide with clouds," I thought when I first shook his willowy hand and gazed up at his welcoming face. It didn't take long to discover that he was towering of mind as well as body. Here was a man of expansive perspectives – someone who took a comprehensive view on life, considering present-day choices with one eye looking back, the other focused forward. He made his living teaching the next generation in the local school. He was also well versed in the ways of the world outside the sunbaked walls of his neighborhood. Beyond the classroom, he educated the public in pop-up street theater performances focused on health and development issues in rural areas. As a regional Scout leader, he guided countless youngsters in the long journey toward building a world that honors both individual and community fulfillment. Once, when I met up with him at a large regional Scout gathering, I noticed how he stood out, even when dressed like everyone else in a sea of khaki uniforms – not because of his height, but because he moved through the crowd with the same embracing grace he radiated when wearing his traditional robes.

I saw Moustapha sporadically over a 15-year period when I traveled to Africa frequently. With every meeting and in the handful of letters I received from him, I had the impression that he treated each facet of tradition like a friend from whom he would never thoughtlessly part. I sensed that when he did feel it was time to relinquish one of the old ways, he would pause, hold it close and memorize how it felt. Then, slowly, mindfully, he'd let go, aware that life would never be quite the same.

It's easy to idealize someone like Moustapha, but there's nothing fanciful about what I gleaned from him. Although we haven't seen nor heard from one another in many years, he enters my mind quite often, usually gliding through in white robes that billow behind him like clouds of contemplation. Whenever he visits my thoughts, I'm reminded of his careful approach to change, and find myself once again considering my own walk toward tomorrow. Is it hasty or thoughtful? Short- or long-sighted? Self-centered or inclusive? I hear his central question on the subject: "Do I understand why

I'm moving from one position to the next, and is it truly a finer place to be?"

Approaching life with a view that material and technological advances should be evolved primarily to create and sustain equality, ecological equilibrium and contemplative space, there was one practice Moustapha held to no matter what else he surrendered: Each morning, when dawn lifted her head above the horizon and glowed with the promise of a new day, in a timeless gesture toward something larger than himself, he bowed until his forehead touched the sand.

NEVER PAY FOR LODGING

You must habit yourself to the dazzle
of the light and of every moment of your life.
Long have you timidly waded
holding a plank by the shore.

~ Walt Whitman

As a Kansas boy reared on a cattle ranch, Kurt rarely felt dazzled by life, but he often felt the satisfaction of hard work and the pride that comes with knowing how to survive in rural America. Time and time again he had sniffed the scent of his own sweat mingling with the musty odors of broad-faced bulls digging in the dirt to raise dust and shield themselves from flies. He grasped the distinction between buying protein from a grocery store and raising one's own beef or hunting and dressing a whitetail deer to feed the family. He understood the reassuring tradition of neighbors helping to haul hay into each other's barns and the pleasure of turning the tractor down its final row just as the sun slips below the horizon and a huge harvest moon raises its golden face in a darkening sky. He also knew the sorrow of standing in a brittle field under a continent of rainless clouds. Not an indoor fellow, he could distinguish the distinct flavor of air in all seasons and circumstances. The *Kansas* air, that is. For he had not tasted a single breath beyond the borders of his home state. It had never even occurred to him – that is, until Richard Burton told him, "It's time."

Not Richard Burton the actor, but Sir Richard Francis Burton, the 19th-century British soldier-explorer-scholar who left a written trail so palpable that it could reach over time and space to touch a fellow coming of age in the American Midwest. It happened in Kurt's last year at Kansas State University, while writing a research paper on Burton for his capstone anthropology class. Here was a subject to make one rethink the scope of his own curiosity and reach!

Burton is said to have spoken 29 languages and traveled enough to use them all. As a 21-year-old in 1842, he aborted his studies at Oxford University, enlisted as a subaltern officer in the East India Company Army, and took up the first of several posts in India. He was an unconventional soldier at every stage of his journey toward becoming a captain. While comrades "dribbled away" spare time playing billiards, he spent untold hours studying India's languages, diving into native customs and religions, tapping his servants for cultural insights, and filling one journal after another with "sights and sounds and smells peculiarly Indian."

His decade in the army cracked open his worldview and set him on voracious pursuits of unbeaten tracks. He ventured to the sacred Muslim cities of Mecca and Medina on the Arabian Peninsula. He became the first European to enter Africa's holy city Harar (Somaliland) and live to tell about it. And he, along with fellow British explorer John Speke, were the first Westerners to see Lake Tanganykia in East Africa. In clothing, as in speech, he usually went native. To win a close look at other worlds, he posed as a gypsy laborer among work gangs on the canals of the Indus River in Sind Province (now part of Pakistan) and as a dervish and wandering holy man when exploring Baluchistan and Punjab. Burton's appearance matched his character. He stood six-feet tall and was wiry strong. The poet Swinburne described him as having the jaw of a devil and the brow of a god. Indeed, he was darkly handsome and fiercely imposing – his bronzed face scarred by a spear wound inflicted by Somali raiders when he was leading an expedition searching for the source of the Nile.

Burton traveled in the old sense of the word; he *travailed.* If he had any fear, it's clear he conquered it with a curiosity so fervent that he returned from every journey with some new measure of enlightenment. His deepest quest was to break any shackles his own culture had placed on him in order to find the essence of existence and the meaning of his role in life. No quick 21st-century adventure tours for him. No collecting showcase mementos of relationships never actually made. No posing beside an anonymous, spear-carrying Maasai in East Africa to have a photo taken. No pictures at all except the images he carried in his mind's eye or recorded with his pen. Beyond writing about his uncommon journeys, discoveries and reflections, Burton brought far-off lands back to Europe by translating extraordinary works such as "Arabian Nights."

The young Kansan who researched Burton's life began his investigation a century after the Englishman died. The effort unleashed a daring desire to see the world and carve an unorthodox path through it, even if it meant loosening his Bible belt. He determined to be a lover of life as *he* discovered it, rather than accepting life packed by someone else. In his capstone paper he proclaimed: "Pursuing the life of Sir Richard Francis Burton has unearthed my own 'voice long stilled.' I feel the wanderlust, the need to touch, taste and feel the world with my own senses. I no longer want to hear of far-off places; I want – and need – to experience them."

He set his sights on Australia. Before leaving, he and his travel mate came to say goodbye to me and his anthropology professor – my husband. They had already started their adventure, working in Nevada mines for several months to save money for their journey. Once in Australia, they would look for work on a cattle ranch – or anywhere. They were both strong Kansas fellows. More than that, they were willing, inquisitive and open-minded. They announced that they had come up with three rules for their journey. Rule #1: Never cower from a new experience. Rule #2: Never pay for lodging. They would have an easygoing attitude, ready to help where needed. If this didn't lead to hospitality in the form of a bed, hammock or hayloft, they would unroll their sleeping bags and slumber under the moon and stars.

As they finished recounting the possibilities of Rule #2, I stirred up a pitcher of iced lemonade and handed each of them a glass. They drank with gusto. "This is the *best* lemonade I've ever had!" said one. "Me too!" said the other. Then I brought out a plate of homemade cookies and passed them around. "These are the *best* cookies of my life!" "Mine too" gushed the other, grinning slyly at his friend. "Okay, what's going on?" I asked. One of them reached for another cookie, held it up and said, "The cookie in your hand *is* the best!" Then he laughed, stuffing the whole thing into his mouth. He had just illustrated Travel Rule #3: Notice what's at hand and celebrate it!

The idea of *carpe diem* or "seize the day" is hardly new, yet I always feel gratefully revitalized when someone comes along and reminds me of it. I relished watching these young men standing poised on the lip of adventure. As a seasoned traveler myself, I knew they were setting out with the most essential gear: Curiosity. Alert, open and teachable, inviting every experience and slighting none, they stood primed for spontaneous appointments with all of life.

After we said goodbye, they climbed into an old pick-up and headed down our gravel road, hands waving out the windows. Just before they rounded the corner, sun struck the dingy truck and for an instant it looked dazzling. I laughed in delight, waving enthusiastically as they disappeared from sight. As I walked back into the house with a skip in my step, I gave a silent thanks for their infectious fervor. And I began to imagine where their sense of wonder might lead them long after this particular trip. Perhaps, after many comings and goings, they would be so tuned to the dazzle of life that they would see it everywhere, even when riding in an old truck on a back road in Kansas.

*

Postscript: We lost touch with Kurt for nearly a decade. Then, in 2004, my husband tracked him down through his minister. The young dreamer we had known in Kansas had become Staff Sergeant Kurt Sayers – a decorated US Army Ranger trained to jump from airplanes, survive in austere environments, handle mountain warfare and provide trauma life support in the field. He had decided to enlist in 2001 while traveling in Thailand, patriotically motivated by the 9/11 terrorist attacks in New York City. Since then, he had carried out dozens of successful combat reconnaissance missions as part of advance force operations in Kosovo, Iraq and Afghanistan. Already, at that early point in his career, his awards and decorations included a Bronze Star, an Army Commendation Medal, a Lifetime Membership in the 75th Ranger Regiment Association (RRA) and a Purple Heart that symbolized the harrowing instant when hot steel ripped into him, and he suffered the loss of an eye.

When Kurt accepted the honor of becoming a lifetime member of the 75th RRA, the premier special operations force within the US Army Special Operations Command, this is part of what he said: *Without doubt, the most critical support we active-duty Rangers receive is in the form of our unit legacy. The daily reminder of our unit heritage, of who we are, who we represent and where we come from. That Ranger tradition is what wills us to run farther, train harder and keep our tomahawks a little sharper. Since World War II, modern Rangers have been at the very forefront of the toughest fighting; 'at the cutting edge of battle.' It is represented in the battle streams of the Regiment, but only truly understood by men who were there.*

And indeed, Kurt was there, time after time, carrying out his younger self's yearning: "I no longer want to hear of far-off places; I want – and need – to experience them."

Recently, as a well-seasoned middle-aged man, Kurt sent a message to my husband, reflecting on his farewell visit with us more than two decades earlier: *I have fond memories of that occasion at your house on the Konza Prairie. It feels like it happened just yesterday. It was the appropriate send off and blessing before we embarked into the unknown to which you and Bunny were familiar. It put the magic of reassurance into our steps, the promise of a safe journey, and the grounding of a realization that it was all very possible, if we just let go a little bit of the known and grasped for the uncertain, whatever and wherever that might be.*

And now, when my couch feels too comfortable or my mirror tells me I'm old, I think of Kurt, recall the launching power of curiosity and rise up primed anew for spontaneous appointments with all of life.

IN THE NEW MOON'S ARMS

A new moon teaches gradualness and deliberation
and how one gives birth to oneself slowly.
Patience with small details makes perfect
a large work, like the universe.
What nine months of attention does for an embryo,
forty early mornings will do for your gradually growing
wholeness.

~ Rumi

"A crescent moon holding its own shadowed fullness." That's how I first described "earthshine" before I knew the term or understood the how and why of this phenomenon, which occurs when sunlight reflects off the Earth and softly illuminates the dark portion of the moon. I penned that description in my journal while stretched out on my sleeping mat in a tent on the southern edge of the Sahara Desert. By day, the desert landscape is an infinite sweep of cerulean sky over endless waves of pale, yellow sand. At night, the scene turns into rolling grey swells beneath a star-splattered indigo sky. Standing in that vast expanse, one can feel lost. But if the eye connects to a star, a planet or the moon, one is suddenly found, inextricably linked to the Universe.

That's how I felt when I saw the earthshine moon. Later I learned that earthshine is also referred to as "the old moon in the new moon's arms."

Several years after seeing earthshine in the Sahara, I saw it in another vast space – the Serengeti Plains of East Africa. I was there writing a story about the problem of local hunters poaching in wildlife sanctuaries. It was the season of the great migration when millions of zebras, wildebeest, and other grazers move across the plains with their newborn calves, following the emergence of fresh pasture. Youngsters stay close to their mothers on this dangerous journey where wild rivers and carnivores claim vulnerable lives. Faced with this spectacle, I couldn't help but think about the cycle of life.

Before I'd left home for this trip, my husband had brought up the idea of having children. We had married three years earlier in our mid-thirties and by then I had cooled to the idea, increasingly pulled to work and the travel that went with it. Wary of giving that up for full-time mothering, I presented all kinds of caveats about co-parenting, turning conversations on the topic into discussions about who would take the kids to piano lessons and swim meets. In some ways, my reticence surprised me. After all, in my teens, I'd preferred babysitting over dating. And in my 20s, I'd relished working at a community center for urban kids. For as long as I could remember, I'd loved being with children. And for many years, I assumed I'd become a mother. Yet, by this time – later in life, in a second marriage and steeped in building a writing career – I had serious reservations about that.

As I looked out on the Serengeti's immense wildlife nursery, those doubts began to feel silly. What, I asked myself, could be more natural than having a family and facing life's wonders and perils together? The question stayed with me throughout that trip. Upon returning home, I described the experience to my husband and with a big smile added this conclusion: "So, yes, let's make a bigger family!" I expected him to say, "Great!" Instead, he asked, "But do you *yearn* for this?" My first thought was, "Really? I've jumped over a hurdle and that's your response?" But then, pausing, I considered his question – both why he asked it and what my answer would be. Talking over the why of it, I learned that he hoped I yearned for motherhood because he didn't want me to feel he was pushing me into it. I told him I didn't feel pushed. I now felt he was opening a door with a prize behind it and inviting me to walk through with him. Thinking out loud, I said, "I don't really feel yearning. I'm deeply happy with my life, with our life. But I know how I am with kids. When and if they come, you won't find a more enthusiastic mother in the neighborhood. And I'd love to know you as a father." It was no stretch of the imagination to picture him in an array of settings with a child. Easiest of all was envisioning him traipsing through the woods with a little person, spontaneously composing tales about forest creatures, building a fire and camping out under the moon and stars. I was convinced that seeing him be a dad would make me love him all the more, and I hoped the same would be true for him seeing me be a mom. Together we concluded that if children came it would be wonderful, and if they didn't it would be another kind of wonderful.

A year later, I was pregnant. The moment we knew for sure, I felt surrounded by an unexpected spaciousness, as if not only my body, but my entire life – our entire lives – were widening to hold an expanding sense of love and purpose. But our celebration was short-lived. After 10 weeks, we lost the baby. Getting back to the idea of a childless kind of wonderful was more difficult than I'd imagined pre-pregnancy. It took time, but gradually we found our way there.

Since it had taken a year to get pregnant, we didn't cling to the idea that it would happen again. But it did. I felt a bit apprehensive to be expecting at age 40, but that emotion soon gave way to joyous anticipation. I began every morning sitting on the couch in our reading loft communing with the tiny being growing inside me – writing in my journal as I considered the qualities of motherhood and childlikeness I was reaching for, picturing myself and the baby in the arms of an intricately interconnected universe that holds all of us in delicate balance. Well before my belly began to swell, we talked happily about the coming new chapter in our lives. Like all parents to be, we discussed names, an endless array of them. Somewhere along the line, we began referring to the baby as "Flint," echoing our love for the Flint Hills of Kansas where we lived at the time. Those rolling, grassy hills, filled with flint stones, exemplified a combination of gentleness and strength that appealed to both of us.

For me, this gestation period – even more than the earlier one – carried an exquisite sense of life unfolding in slow motion. As the months rolled by, it felt like a time of patient becoming, like watching a time-exposure film of a bud forming and opening. . .

But the film stopped before the flower bloomed. Five-and-a-half months into the pregnancy, I went to my obstetrician's office for a routine checkup. We had met three times before, and I'd delighted in our conversations about parenting and the volunteer neo-natal work she did with women in developing countries. However, she was abroad during this visit, so one of her colleagues met with me. Immediately, I sensed his clinical manner and missed her warmth, her graciousness. *Perhaps he's having a rough day*, I thought, trying to remain positive as he carried out his examination with detached professionalism. After doing an ultrasound and sliding his stethoscope around on my belly, he announced that he couldn't find a heartbeat.

There was no heartbeat.

Hearing his words, I was numb, speechless. Then, he said something profoundly odd and disturbing: "I suppose you just want to get the damn thing out." Dazed by his cruel delivery of that heart piercing news, I was barely conscious of him walking me to the receptionist to schedule an appointment to remove Flint from my body as soon as possible. Taking the appointment card, I turned and walked out the door, somehow sensing that I wouldn't return.

I called my husband, who quickly left his office at the university to meet me at home. Hand-in-hand, we took a long slow walk along the lake nestled between the hills by our home. We said little. What could we say? It was a conversation of hand squeezes, punctuated by embraces and long pauses of leaning into one another while gazing out over the lake.

I spent the next day tending the garden, feeling the need to help something grow. As I weeded and watered, I saw my beloved making his way into the woods on a path just below the raised bed where I was working. He had a shovel in his hand. Without him having to tell me, I knew he was going to dig a little grave – a tough task in the flinty Kansas soil. I knew where it would be: In a spot under a sprawling wild rosebush, alongside the resting places of two of our cats and a wild fox that he had buried in previous years. That evening, from our collection of baskets, gifted or purchased over years of working with Native Americans in Maine, he chose a round one made of sweetgrass and wood strips, and lined it with soft grass in preparation.

The following afternoon, contractions started. By nightfall, they became intense, and I asked my husband to read me passages from sacred texts we have in our home. These included an old hymn titled "Mother's Evening Prayer," which begins with the words, "Oh gentle presence...." When the tiny being passed through me, his father gathered him up and placed him in the basket he'd prepared. Then he ran a warm bath for me, kissed me and went out to the woods.

Lying in the soothing water, I pictured him in the woodland clearing under dappled moonlight. When he returned, his arms and hands were covered with dirt, and he was holding a book. Sitting on the edge of the tub, he said, "I thought I should read something at the gravesite on your behalf, so I took a Bible and flashlight with me. I opened the book randomly, and my eyes fell upon this passage: 'He led you through the great and terrible wilderness and brought water for you out of the rock of flint' (Deut. 8:15)."

How was it possible, I wondered, that he landed on those words? They felt like a promise. Like a promise of water in a desert. Like a promise that the small bit of mothering and fathering we'd experienced through Flint had already blessed our lives. When we finally went to bed, I held to that idea as my husband held me in his arms and we wearily found our way to slumber.

The next morning, we agreed that he should go to work for a couple of hours – to teach his class of 400 anthropology students. Somehow, I pictured them as a room-full of Flints awaiting nurturing. When he left, I went to our reading loft, the place where I'd communed daily with Flint. Sitting there, I prayed and wrote in my journal, sorting my way through all that had transpired. Here, in part, is what came to me:

We have not lost Flint. . . . His identity remains intact and continues to bless. This pregnancy awakened me to the joys of a new kind of discipline, of nurturing, of glimpsing the spiritual essence of life, of feeling my oneness with God and Her many manifestations, and of seeing even more loving qualities in the man I married. I want to claim those blessings and embrace the idea that not only is Flint intact, but my motherhood – the attributes of mothering that have been revealed over the past half year – are unbroken and will continue to bless my life, my work, my family.

Beyond and encircling this Earthly home, Flint and I both reside in the womb of God, the universal, nurturing Life Force. There is a continuity of good in this experience, provided I don't abort it – cut it out of my life – but rather strive to cultivate motherhood through tenderness, nobility, strength, selflessness, service, resilience, spontaneity, productivity. . .

I'm thinking of a stanza from the hymn, "Mother's Evening Prayer": "No snare no fowler, pestilence or pain, no night drops down upon the troubled breast when heaven's aftersmile Earth's teardrop gains, and mother finds her home and heavenly rest." What is the "aftersmile" – the rainbow – of this downpour of tears? I think it is the assurance that there is a home for my mothering qualities that may not be realized with children of our "own" but perhaps in other wondrous ways. In the big picture, what appears to be loss may reveal itself as an unimagined gain. Take the wheat of this experience and burn the tares. True healing is not about enduring suffering and gaining stamina, but rather it is about transforming suffering and adversity into a blessing. Like Jacob, hold to the angel of this experience until it blesses you.

Looking at those journal pages today, so many years later, they seem prescient. My life is abundantly blessed with young people – nephews, nieces, a goddaughter, former students – and so much more. Those who have raised children of their own will no doubt think I feel this way because I don't know what I'm missing. I suspect that's true – which is a blessing in itself. So, too, are my pregnancies, even though they ended too soon. Looking back, I see that they led to a different kind of birthing than I'd anticipated: My own gradual growing into wholeness and an awareness of the infinite manifestations of what it means to be whole. Carrying babes within me – especially the longer journey with Flint – lit my life in ways I could not have imagined.

I still feel held by the light of that experience – like an old moon in a new moon's arms.

(Note: Our experience of going through a stillbirth at home without a doctor or midwife was not planned. It came upon us quickly, and we did not realize the serious risk involved. The fact that it went smoothly with no complications does not mean that I'm recommending this for others.)

WITHOUT THINKING OF THERE

Now we will count to twelve and we will all keep still
for once on the face of the earth. . . . ~ Pablo Neruda

On New Year's Eve 1999, even the moon held back her appearance until midnight had safely passed. All around the world people greeted that night with varying degrees of apprehension. On the clock's twelfth chime, the twentieth century and the second millennium would come to an end. The year 2000 held totemic significance. More apocalyptic predictions were connected to it than to any other point in recorded history. The array of doomsayers for this moment in time was remarkable. It ranged from 13th century theologian Peter Olivi to19th-century Theosophical Society founder Helena Blavatsky and modern-day Christian leaders including televangelist Jerry Falwell. Christian psychic Ruth Montgomery also weighed in, proclaiming that the Earth's axis would shift, and the Antichrist would reveal himself that year.

Forebodings were fueled by a global computer glitch that threatened to change life as we knew it. The problem sprang from early computing days when programmers established a date system based on the last two digits of the year. This meant that when 1999 gave way to 2000, many of the world's computers would read it as 1900. People worried that, at that moment, systems worldwide would crash, causing major catastrophes. Alternately referred to as the Millennium Bug and the Y2K (Year 2000) Problem, the threat appeared especially troubling for major industries – utilities, banking, manufacturing, telecom and airlines. The U.S. Secretary of Defense described its potential danger as the "electronic equivalent of the El Niño."

Well in advance of the new calendar, governments and industries around the globe began hustling to patch the faulty date-handling code to make all systems "Y2K Compliant." New York City alone spent more than $300 million in preparation and then held Year 2000 drills with all its agencies participating in imagined crisis scenarios.

By December 31st, in a poll asking New Yorkers if the Millennium Bug made them concerned about going out on New Year's Eve, half said "not at all." Yet only 15 percent said they would venture out that night. All across the country a majority of Americans said they expected to face the New Year at home with family and friends. Of those planning to turn on a TV and watch the famous ball drop down the flagpole at Times Square, half expected their screens would go black the moment the countdown reached zero.

Amid all the speculation, my husband Harald suggested an alternative New Year's Eve plan: "Let's camp overnight in the hills someplace where we can't see a single wire or light or any other sign of human habitation or technology." I didn't have winter camping experience, but I liked the idea a lot. Temperatures in Kansas were predicted to be in the low 20s, which, with a tent and down sleeping bags, seemed quite doable.

Harald left home around noon to set up camp on our friend's 400-acre stretch of land in the rolling Flint Hills. While he was gone, I turned off and unplugged our computers, disconnected digital household gadgets, and put together a basket of foodstuffs.

We set out after nightfall with our cat Madockawando in tow. Like all his predecessors in our household, he had an American Indian name – his came from a 17th-century Wabanaki grand chief in Maine. However, because this particular cat was more comical than chiefly, we called him Ijsco, the Dutch word for ice cream. From the time he was a kitten, he had behaved like a dog in feline disguise, so we often took him hiking with us. Bright white, he was easy to locate. If the civilized world fell apart at midnight, we figured he'd be safer with us in the techno-free hills than back at the house alone.

Reaching our friend's land, I jumped out of the car to open and close the gate. Once I was back in, Harald drove as far as possible along a rutted track, then stopped and said, "We'll have to walk the rest of the way." He switched off the engine and the headlights, leaving us engulfed in blackness. I scanned the sky, searching for the moon. Totally out of sight, it offered no help. But with our flashlights and my husband's keen sense of direction, we found our way to the campsite.

Harald had prepared everything between the arms of a dry riverbed just to be sure our campfire wouldn't set the fields aflame. He'd laid kindling and firewood within a circle of stones. On one side of the circle, he'd built two chairs using slabs of limestone, which are ubiquitous in this landscape. On the other, he'd positioned several more slabs as heat reflectors to keep us warm. Best of all, he'd gathered a huge pile of leaves and placed our two-person tent atop it. Stepping inside, I unzipped both of our sleeping bags, laid one on top of the other, and then unrolled my luxurious surprise: the goose down comforter from our bed. We would have a cozy night's sleep even if the temperature dropped lower than expected.

Meanwhile, Harald tended to the fire – one of his favorite activities. Ijsco was nowhere to be seen. But when the fire gained strength and created a circle of light, I caught a glimpse of him in a nearby tree, perched on a limb like a snowy owl. A moment later, he shinnied down the trunk and disappeared into the darkness. Periodically, as we worked, he returned to the campsite, romped around us, and then gallivanted off.

When the fire became glowing hot, we propped a grill rack over it and began roasting our dinner of steak, tomatoes and potatoes. Already rubbed with herbs in the kitchen back home, our meal savorized the air and made me feel ravenous. We ate with our hands, licking the juices from our fingers. Ijsco came by for some meat and then disappeared again.

For dessert, I pulled out a thermos of cocoa and unwrapped two big cookies. Leaning back on our limestone chairs, we talked unhurriedly about life – work, family, places we wanted to travel, art we'd like to make, books we hoped to write. We reminisced about our early days together in New York and marveled how, hailing from opposite sides of the ocean, we'd found each other amid millions of people in the city. He told me things I needed to hear, and I did the same. We mused about the best and worst events of the first and second millenniums and speculated whether the third would be more peaceful. We talked about hopes for the coming year and beyond – for ourselves and the world. His eyes were bright and attentive in the firelight – and I like to think that mine were too. In that halo of light, everything hoped for seemed possible. Above our heads, stars flickered like distant campfires. But the moon had yet to show her face.

Every now and then, we added more wood to the fire and then gradually let it ember down. We had no idea of the time – neither one of us ever wears a watch and I'd left my new flip phone at home. But when a coyote howled, we took that as our signal that 1999 had come to an end. "Happy New Year!" we said simultaneously. Then, out of nowhere, Ijsco scampered into camp. All three of us were ready for the tent. Slipping inside, we zipped the door flap shut and settled in for a deep sleep. A moment later Harald said, "Is this the down comforter from our bed?"

Cozy and utterly content in our downy nest, I thought of the opening line of a poem I'd read long before: "Shall I stay here and think of there or go there and think of here?" I realized there was no place I'd rather be at that moment and basked in the sense of feeling fully present exactly where I was. I pulled Harald in close and whispered, "Thank you."

We woke up just after dawn to a clear cold day. After rebuilding the fire, we brewed tea, warmed up scones and celebrated the fact that at least our wilderness world had survived the New Year's arrival. Looking up, I saw the moon in third-quarter phase – a tilted smile in the ice blue sky. In my imagination, it was a smile of relief.

Back home, we reconnected all electronics. Everything worked. Turning on the radio, I heard that the world was still intact. As it turned out, after watching the year 2000 move across Asia and Europe with few significant Y2K-related problems, a record-breaking crowd had gathered at Times Square in New York City to greet the New Year. There was a brief pregnant pause when the countdown reached zero. Then, when the world around them didn't explode, everyone cheered and cheered.

Still, I looked at my computer warily and avoided the lures of email and the Internet all day. Not because I expected my devices to blow up in my face. Rather because I had felt so content during our short but complete break from it and other modern technologies. Wrapped up in nature on a night of global digital distraction and apprehension, we had greeted the New Year with a curious feeling of being cleansed. Little did I realize then how modest that cleanse was compared to what would be needed in the years ahead when smart phones and digital social platforms would transform humankind's ways of being in the world. I don't usually make New Year resolutions, but on 1 January 2000, profoundly grateful for Harald's gift of a New Year's Eve surrounded by nature and free from devices, I made a vow. I promised myself to unplug regularly for meaningful stretches of time, not because of technology scares, but to maintain a relationship with stillness and to make sure I never forget how to single-task in a sea of multi-tasking – how to give full attention without interruption to conversations by a campfire, to the pure call of a coyote, to the sheer elegance of a morning moon.

THE PRAYER OF YES

There is a life force within your soul;
seek that life.
There is a gem in the mountain of your body;
seek that mine.

~ Rumi

Some years ago, darkness came over me like a lunar eclipse. It began in the winter months with a vague gloominess that I assumed would just go away. But by the time spring arrived, it had become worse. As the days grew longer and life all around me reached toward renewal, I felt like a plant shriveling in a shadow. At night, I slept fitfully or not at all. Come daybreak, I was a sloth on a slow day. I could barely get out of bed.

I was away from home, guest teaching at a small midwestern college. Three weeks into the semester, when I'd sunk to what felt like my lowest point, my Swiss friend Pierre, a sociologist who'd spent two decades working on rural development issues in West Africa, arrived to give a lecture. I don't recall the topic, but most likely it included his conviction that no development project can succeed unless love is the major motivation behind it. That's what he thought and what he lived – this man who divides his paycheck in three: a third to live on, a third to save, a third to give away. Pierre notices the needs of others. He feels compelled to help meet them. He's the kind of friend who calls forth your empathy toward all life by example, not instruction. He leaves a deep imprint on hearts and a light footprint on Earth – getting about on foot, bike or public transportation and surviving on a plant-based diet prepared raw to avoid unnecessary energy consumption. The books and articles he writes are about living simply, listening deeply, finding your true spiritual path and building social justice.

Soon after arriving on campus, Pierre phoned and asked me to take a walk with him. Normally, any opportunity for us to spend time together filled me with joy. Now, despite the promise of discovery that every visit with him held, I barely mustered the will to say yes.

Leaving campus on foot, we made our way upward through fields toward the lip of towering limestone bluffs that overlook the majestic Mississippi River. Pierre is not a long-legged man, but he ascended the sloped backside of the bluffs as if he were, taking great strides, his bearded head leaning into the hill as if we were climbing his homeland alps. When we reached the top of the ridge, the sprawling drama of the river and its mosaic backdrop of farm fields came into view. As we walked along the winding ridge, I didn't speak of my misery, but I knew Pierre sensed it because ever so gradually, he slowed his brisk pace. When we came to an especially lovely lookout point, he stopped, turned toward me and asked if I knew about the "Prayer of Yes." I didn't, so he told me. He said it was a simple practice. All you do is go about your day consciously looking for what you can say yes to – and when you find something, you say *Yes*. Out loud. I watched as he faced the vista and said *YES*.

Lying in bed the next morning, I buried my head under the comforter, resisting the start of yet another miserable day. Alone with my thoughts in that dark cocoon, I thought about Pierre and his "Prayer of Yes." Some minutes passed. Tentatively, I pulled back the cover just enough to peek out. The window shades were drawn, but I saw a crack of light along the bottom edges. After a long pause, I whispered, *Yes* to the rising sun. One of the windows was partly open, and a breeze wafted through, slightly lifting the shade and revealing a bit more light. *Yes,* I said to the uplifting wind. Then I noticed birdsong. *Yes,* to singing for no apparent reason. Pulling myself up from bed, I ambled to the shower, stepped in and sighed, *Yes*, to the cascade of warm water sliding down my body. Later, biking to campus, I passed my favorite tree. *Yes,* to that sturdy sky-reaching friend.

I turned down Lilac Lane and drank in the scent – *Yes*. In class, I found students eager to learn, and I could say *Yes* to the pull toward knowledge and understanding. And so it went throughout the day. There were many emotional slumps, but I yessed my way through them.

Walking home in night's stillness, I said *Yes* to the serenity I longed for. Passing the lilacs again – *Yes* to them smelling even sweeter under moonlight. Taking note of the moon, I said *Yes* to that calm radiant presence. I became aware of a rhythm in all those yesses, a kind of musical beat that energized the movement of mind and body.

The following morning, I felt a slight bit of relief. It was barely perceptible, but enough to prompt me to practice the Prayer of Yes again that day… and the next… Within a week or two, I noticed that finding more to say yes to had become a lifeline of connection. Then it occurred to me that what I was saying yes to was Life itself, with its innumerable expressions. Was I one of those expressions? Was I being breathed forth by a Universal Life Force? I began to sense that each *Yes* was a shining ray casting light on Life's beauty and purpose. In time, I grew so attuned to the light held in each *Yes* that I could sense it dissipating the darkness that had enveloped me.

As I experienced the gloom dissolving, I wondered what had caused it and why it had grown from a thin grey pall into something so dark and dense. Had it come from feeling closed in on a small, remote campus? Was it the world's countless conflicts and sorrows pressing in on my heart? The deep hole of an old emotional wound never fully filled? Could it be a question of diet or chemical imbalance? Or might it be something totally unexpected, such as an ignored garden of blessings demanding to be noticed and tended?

The last idea in that inventory of musings took me by surprise. It felt intriguing, liberating, and eclipsed all the others. I sat with it for a while. Rather than looking for some situational or psychological cause for my entrenched heavy-heartedness, I suddenly saw my misery as a clarion call to seek out its opposite. It was as if the shadows were shouting, *Look behind me; what do you see? – Light!* As if questions were answers pulling me toward the full measure of my being, inviting me to tune into and turn toward the underlying wholeness and splendor of Life. Then came the idea that the Prayer of Yes could involve more than nodding at the obviously good natural wonders, people and events that crossed my path. What if I also said *Yes* to the pits, boulders and snags along the way – to whatever trips me up, slows me down and prompts me to recalculate my route? What if I journeyed forward expectantly, open to learning from *whatever* comes my way? What if, every time the path was dark, rough and cold, I told the Universe, *Yes, okay, this, too, is part of the human experience and the journey of discovery that is the hallmark of our species. I say Yes to this. I say Yes to what it has to tell me. I say Yes to Life.*

And so it went. Gradually, the Prayer of Yes in all its incarnations helped shift my gaze away from the shadow – the belief that I was an isolated being disconnected from that Universal Life Force. It turned me toward the light of my essential being as part of a wondrous whole. And therein, I found serenity and a source of deep, durable joy.

I cannot end this story without saying a direct *Yes* to Pierre for being so fully who he was that day on the bluffs and for remaining so all these years since. During our many decades of friendship, I've watched him foster social justice and spiritual growth in his global circle of compassion – whether working with nongovernmental organizations, teaching workshops, advocating for prison reform, or writing books rich with stories and insights that awaken hearts and minds. Well after that springtime walk, Pierre wrote a book titled, *The Gentle Art of Blessing*. It includes a line that echoes what I gleaned from him through the Prayer of Yes: "On awakening, bless this day, for it is already full of unseen good which your blessing will call forth, for to bless is to acknowledge the unlimited good that is embedded in the texture of the universe and awaiting each and all."

BEING TOGETHER

There is no harmony
when everyone plays the same note.
                                    ~ Neil Millar

I am always in the hope to express the love of two
lovers by a marriage of two complementary colors,
their mingling and their opposition,
the mysterious vibrations of kindred tones.
                                    ~ Vincent van Gogh

Justus the cellist and Margaretha the clairvoyant had one
of the best marriages I've ever witnessed. They lived in
a small studio on the top floor of Amsterdam's sprawling
Carlton Hotel – previously an apartment building. All the
other rooms in that grand art deco building hosted a
rotation of transient visitors. Justus and Margaretha were
the only permanent residents, thanks to a lawyer friend
who secured their private space when a luxury hotel
chain purchased and transformed the building in 1985.
They stayed put during the renovation, a cacophony of
change that altered everything except their one-room
home and its spectacular view. It retained the character

it had when they moved there in 1953, three years into their marriage.

When they wed, Justus was 23 and Margaretha 42. They were an unusual pair – not only because she was two decades older than he, but because he was shy, steady and self-effacing, while she was outspoken, temperamental and exuberantly social.

Born into a patrician family, Margaretha grew up in a grand town house. Then, as the story goes, her father died in a duel. After his death, her mother learned that he'd gambled away everything and left them in debt. She threw his pistols in the canal and moved into a tiny apartment with her lithe and lively daughter. Just out of high school, Margaretha began working at a pharmaceutical company to support them. Their bank account may have plummeted, but her confidence did the opposite. Capitalizing on her elite education and holding on to her upper-class manners and connections, she enjoyed a vibrant social life, organizing house concerts in other people's salons and entertaining a string of society suitors. One of them, a well-known glider pilot, often took her out riding in his chic, open-top Hispano-Suiza sportscar. (Her driving cap ended up in the national museum.) That relationship came to a woeful end during WWII, when he died in a German concentration camp. By then, Margaretha had taken a job as assistant to a famous psychiatrist in Amsterdam. His work fascinated her, given her own interest in the mental world. She considered herself clairvoyant and often used Tarot cards and astrology charts to offer guidance to friends, most of whom found her unusual insights fascinating and helpful and often came back for more. She believed in fate, and reading her own situation, proclaimed she had no doubt that "there's someone I'll meet who is 'mine.'"

Justus' father was a medical doctor with artistic roots in the Dutch province of Friesland, where his grandfather and great uncles are still heralded for the role their poetry and fiction played in the development of a written literature in the Frisian language. (One of them, Eeltsje Halbertsma, penned the Frisian national anthem.) Justus' mother, who came from a family of musicians and attorneys, died when he was just two years old. A punishing stepmother stomped into her place and squashed his self-confidence. He grew up thinking he was "nothing" and that the only antidote to that was to be perfectly brilliant at whatever he did, especially at playing the cello, his passion. Aiming high and certain that he was missing that mark, he felt perpetually inadequate. When his first love left him, his sense of worthlessness reached such proportions that he could no longer pick up his bow. His stepmother, dismissive of what she saw as weakness, could muster no comfort.

Finally, in 1947 at age 21, desperate to end what he called his "dauerdepression" (permanent depression), Justus sought help from a Freudian analyst. Years later, looking back at this time in his life, he said that in the very first session, he knew he had found a person who offered him something no one else ever had: a sympathetic, insightful insistence to look at himself and his life circumstances with bold honesty, not to moralize or judge but to identify and discard whatever held him down. It was an intense, three-year journey, but within that time, Justus found his courage and dignity, reunited with his cello, began studying at the music conservatory – and met Margaretha.

Their paths crossed in 1949 during his last year of treatment. It happened in a canal house where students rented rooms. Margaretha had gone there to visit a friend and, upon arrival, saw Justus coming down the stairs. He was young, lanky and handsome in a sensitive, slightly awkward, poetic kind of way. Immediately, she recognized him as that "one who is 'mine.'" For her, it was love at first sight. She pursued him . . . and he succumbed, drawn by her radiance, certainty and experience. She had a full life behind her. His was just beginning. Yet, at this crossroads in their lives, each recognized in the other something they yearned for. A year later, they exchanged marriage vows and ventured off on a shared path.

For all the contrasts in their personalities and life experiences, Justus and Margaretha had a fair amount in common and much that was complementary. He was devoted to playing the cello. She was an enthusiastic, knowledgeable, and well-connected devotee of the musical arts, who celebrated and helped facilitate his efforts toward becoming a professional musician. It's hard to say which one of them was more thrilled when he won a seat in the Netherlands Ballet Orchestra, which accompanies the Dutch National Opera and Ballet in Amsterdam and on international tours. Margaretha dominated their conversations and decisions, but she adored Justus and always waited up for him when he came home from performances – presenting him with a simple meal and ears eager to hear every detail. Both had eccentricities. He didn't like buttons on his vests or sweaters, so she cut them all off and sewed on hooks. She was inclined to make decisions based on the stars, and he went along. When it came to material needs and wants, both of them were minimalists. What they cared about had to do with mind, soul, art. Contented Bohemians, they surrounded themselves with a circle of likeminded friends – writers, musicians, artists and intellectuals, many of them well-known.

My first encounter with Margaretha and Justus happened in the 1980s, when she was in her late 70s and he in his late 50s. We met through my Dutch husband Harald, whose parents were long-time friends with them. Margaretha had opened the door to their friendship years earlier, approaching my father-in-law in a café shortly after he'd returned from six months of anthropological fieldwork in Kenya. She walked up to his table, introduced herself and asked why he was tan mid-winter and what he was writing in his notebook.

As Harald and I made our way to their apartment for that first introduction, he warned me about Margaretha's clairvoyance. Convinced that she could see right through people, she would likely decide on the spot whether or not she liked me. I knew from my mother-in-law that Margaretha had told her, "Harald is an eagle who needs to be free and will not survive if he's caged." As Margaretha saw it, being committed to one person would break his spirit. So, I was slightly concerned she might balk at our serious relationship – even though I was as averse to caging someone as I was to being caged myself. As it turned out, I need not have worried. Within minutes of our arrival, I felt welcomed by her. Perhaps she saw ease in our eyes, or maybe she was feeling generous because she and Justus had just celebrated their wedding anniversary and their own love filled the air.

Whatever the reason for Margaretha's apparent acceptance of my presence, soon after introductions, Harald and Justus stepped into the kitchenette to make tea, and she headed to the couch. Sitting down, she patted the space beside her, summoning me to join her. She had a little book in her hand and told me Justus had written it in celebration of their anniversary. "I'll read it to you," she proclaimed, opening it on her lap so I could see the handwritten text. Page one professed, "Dearest Margaretha, I loved you yesterday." She turned to page two: "And I love you today." Then to page three: "And I will love you tomorrow." Followed by page 4: "And the next day." Then to page 5: "And the next." So it continued, page after page – at least twenty of them – until the final one, where "the next day" became "forever."

"This must be your favorite book," I said, laughing.

"And by my favorite author," she replied.

In the years that followed, Harald and I rarely missed stopping by Justus and Margaretha's place during our regular trips to the Netherlands. I felt drawn to them for many reasons, especially for the way their notable differences always seemed to manifest as complementarity rather than conflict. I wondered how that could be. Was it hard work for them to find their fit?

Were both or one of them consciously and constantly adjusting to avoid clashing? Were they repressing their real feelings? Eventually, I came to the simple conclusion that the ease I saw in their relationship sprang from their acceptance of and appreciation for the distinct qualities each brought to their union, combined with a conviction that despite appearances, they were kindred spirits who belonged together. There was never a hint that they fought their differences, and that has been a beacon for my own marriage.

When we tapped on their door in 2001, it was Justus who answered. He invited us in with a soft voice and led us to the hospital bed he'd rented so he could care for Margaretha at home after doctors said there was nothing more they could do. She was now in her 90s and he in his 70s. They had been together for half a century, and both wanted more.

The four of us chatted a bit, and then Justus led me to the sweep of windows that overlooked the city, while Harald stayed by Margaretha. Side by side in silence, we gazed out at the heart of historic Amsterdam. I now knew the landmarks without him telling me. To the north we could see the New Church (originally built in the 15th century) and just west of it the Westerkerk where Rembrandt lies, and to the southwest the famous Rijksmuseum. Just below the windows, the city's famous flower market was rolled out like a colorful carpet under watery gray skies. As always, although it was a wet winter day, the windows were open slightly to let in fresh air. After a minute or two, I said what seemed obvious, aiming to open a space for Justus to talk if he wished to: "Caring for her all by yourself must be so difficult." When he responded, "No, we're together," I sensed that was all he wanted to say about her illness. Silence returned for a while, and then I asked, "Justus, do you have a favorite cello piece?"

"That's a difficult question. There are so many beautiful ones."

"But if you had to choose just one?"

"It would be Gabrielli's Sonata in A major."

"Would you play it for us?"

He looked down at his hands and then apologetically at me: "My hands aren't very good right now. But I think I have a recording of it by Anner Bylsma. I'll look for it." He walked to the shelves at the end of the room, rummaged around and then, looking pleased, waved a CD in the air. He placed the disk in the CD player but didn't turn it on. "First, I'll make tea, and then we'll listen," he said, stepping into the kitchenette.

A few minutes later Justus appeared with the tea tray. He placed it on a stool beside Margaretha's bed and arranged a little semi-circle of seats for the three of us.

We sat down, he filled our cups, and we talked as we sipped. When my cup was half empty, he stood up and leaned over Margaretha to place a sound amplifier on her head. Then he joyfully announced, "We're going to have music!"

She smiled.

As Justus moved toward the CD player to switch it on, I noticed a rolled-up mat and folded sheets under the bed. I pictured him pulling out the bundle nightly to sleep near his wife. When he rejoined us, the sonata's first movement, *Grave,* had begun, filling the room with melancholic yearning. He sat down and closed his eyes. Soon, yearning gave way to a light-hearted chase for joy in the *Allegro*, and Justus' fingertips began dancing along the frets of a cello in his mind. During the reflective *Largo* that followed, he reached over to Margaretha and touched her hand.

*

The day Margaretha died, Justus held her in his arms well past the moment she took her last breath. When he finally let her go, he followed her wish and arranged for her to be cremated. She had also asked that he release her ashes in the northern rural part of the country where they'd always spent their holidays biking – and where they first met my father-in-law. Justus waited until late spring and then took the train north with his bike and

Margaretha's remains. Upon arrival, he peddled five kilometers to my husband's family home. We were there at the time, intentionally present for this final farewell.

The next morning, my husband, brother-in-law and I picked an array of blossoms and flower petals from the garden, filling a large basket. Come mid-morning, we and several others gathered with Justus at the head of a woodland trail that led to an open field of wild grasses peppered with tiny purple orchids. Reaching the field, we made our way to a place where two meandering streams meet and flow into a river still known by its ancient name, the *Aa*. We stood there on the shore with Justus as he collected his thoughts. I assumed he would speak. Instead, he carefully opened the container that held Margaretha's ashes, lifted it as surely and gracefully as if it were his bow, and cast the ephemeral traces of his wife into the air. At that very moment, a gust of wind flew in and lifted them skyward. In unified surprise, all of us uttered a hushed *ohhh!* The cloud of ashes hung there for an instant before drifting down to the water. Then, Justus took a handful of flower petals from the basket by his feet and tossed them toward the remnants. One by one, each of us did the same, offering him our condolences as we sent Margaretha on her way in a moving bed of blooms.

Just downstream, a small footbridge arched over the slender, slow-moving river. After adding our petals to the flow, each of us ambled in that direction, until Justus stood alone where the streams met. From our vantage point on the bridge, we observed him watching the trail of flowers as they floated toward us. A few minutes passed before he walked in our direction, joining us just in time to see the tail end of that trail slip under the bridge. Then all of us turned around, eyes fixed on the flowers until they disappeared where the river bends on its way to the sea.

THE MEASURE OF A LIFE

The best cure for weariness is helping someone
who is even more tired.
~ Gordon B. Hinckley

Last night as I was sleeping, I dreamt . . .
golden bees were making . . . sweet honey
from my old failures.
~ Antonio Machado

Sarah's story has more twists and turns than one of her woodsplint baskets. It took her a long time to weave her life into wholeness.

I first started visiting Sarah at her home in northern Maine to record her oral history as part of the research for the Aroostook Band of Micmacs' federal recognition and land claim case. Like many Native American groups, the Micmac[1] had no formal status as Indians in the United States. None of their ancestral land in northern Maine had been secured, and they lacked the health and education benefits that federally recognized tribes have. Most band members lived in poverty and

---

[1] Now spelled Mi'kmaq

93

survived by doing migrant labor and making baskets out of wood stripped from the trunks of brown ash trees.

When I met Sarah, I was emerging from a difficult period in my own life. Because of my struggles, I found myself listening to her not only with anthropological ears in search of Native history and cultural patterns, but with a human heart in search of perspective, hope and answers.

I went to see Sarah often, at first for work, but then, as time went by, also for the pleasure of friendship. We talked in her kitchen, her vegetable garden, or in her living room where she did her weaving. Her home always smelled delicious – a mix of freshly scraped ash splints and something savory cooking on the stove. No matter how busy she was, she always made time for me – and always served food.

Sarah's life began in 1927 at the small Eel River Bar reservation situated on the Bay of Chaleur near Dalhousie, New Brunswick, the Canadian province that borders northern Maine. Her mother was a basketmaker, her father a fur-trapper and seasonal laborer. Soon after Sarah's birth, her dad built a remote log cabin in the woods just across the bay on the south shore of Gaspe Peninsula and took his family there.

Sarah's earliest memory was of her mother calling for help: "When I was a tiny girl," she told me, "Mama was sick. She used to holler, *Sarah, go get my pail!* and she would vomit blood into it. When I was just four-and-a-half, she died. At her wake, I crawled into her casket. I'd always slept with her, and I thought it was a fancy bed. My father gave me the worst spanking of my life at that wake."

More loss came for Sarah at age seven. That was the year her father delivered her to the Indian Residential School at Shubenacadie, Nova Scotia, and ventured off on his own to make a living. Like other children at the boarding school, Sarah was punished if she spoke Micmac – straps on the hand and bed without supper. Within a year, she had lost her Native tongue.

In 1941, when Sarah was 14, her father became ill, and she was pulled from school to look after him. Once she had nursed him back to health, he set out again to pursue his livelihood, and Sarah moved in with an army widow who needed help with her seven kids. It was the first of many caretaking and housekeeping jobs she would have in her lifetime.

The following year, Sarah left that job to work for a wealthy couple who lived just three miles from her home reservation. Longing to be with her own people, she walked there whenever she could get away. During one visit, she met Abe Harquail, a Micmac fur trapper who stayed on the reservation at his sister's house between hunting expeditions. Abe reminded Sarah of her father. Drawn to the familiar, she married him a year later. He was 33, she was 15.

The day after her 16th birthday, Sarah gave birth to a son. A second son and a daughter came in quick succession. Before long, Abe quit his solo trapping life, and like many Micmacs of the day, he and Sarah took up a migratory existence with their young kids in tow. Sarah described it like this: "From April through May we'd be living on the reserve digging clams in Dalhousie. During June and July, we'd make potato baskets, usually in Maine. In August, we raked blueberries in Maine, and in September and October, we worked the potato harvest there. If we found a good rent after the harvest, we'd stay till March."

As migrant laborers in that era, they knew about lousy, makeshift accommodations in leaky barns, dilapidated shacks and drafty potato storage houses. Yet, as Sarah often said, "I could turn any place into a home." She was a unique sort of homebody, someone who carried home in her heart and hands and created it no matter where she landed. She'd gather wildflowers, prepare a delicious stew over an open fire, and attract songbirds with breadcrumbs. Also, she radiated a distinct kind of elegance, even when dressed in jeans and a flannel shirt. It had to do with the way she tilted her chin upward as if cajoling the clouds to part; the way her dark hair waved loosely around high cheeks and straight shoulders; the fluid movement of her strong arms and fingers when gardening, cooking or weaving. She was petite but had a long easy stride and walked like she knew where she was going. She was a free spirit, always up for an adventure. And she liked moving around with Abe. He was the one true love of her life.

But. There was a tragic flaw in their union. In her words: "Abe's alcoholism was something awful. He used to beat me so bad and leave me for months at a time. I tried to work when he was gone, but I had three kids, and it was hard." It was also hard for Abe. His addiction was a disease implanted generations earlier when American Indians first encountered European fishers and fur traders who introduced them to alcohol and often got them drunk to cheat them in trade deals.

In 1949, after Abe disappeared on yet another drinking binge, Sarah did something she swore she'd never do, no matter how desperate: She abandoned her children, delivering her two boys to the Indian boarding school where her father had left her and placing her little daughter in the care of a friend. Then she left Abe.

Needing refuge, Sarah went back to the reservation where she had family and friends. Eventually, on an evening out in the nearby port of Dalhousie, she met a Norwegian sea captain whose freight ship was docked there. By the time he pulled up anchor, they had decided to stay in touch through letters.

Sarah began going to northern Maine for seasonal labor again, and after one potato harvest, she chose to stay on in Limestone, where she found a job at the local taxi stand. Her sea captain came looking for her, and in 1952 she married him. They honeymooned in Japan. He bought her a home in Limestone. Whenever possible, she joined him at various ports. In 1955, she met him in San Francisco with happy news that she was pregnant with his child. But when she returned home, she miscarried. Just a couple of months later, she received devastating news that her husband had been killed instantly when his ship, loaded with mining explosives, blew up. For more than a year after those twin sorrows, Sarah lived aimlessly, going through the motions of her job at the taxi stand, feeling lost in an expanding hole of emptiness.

Still young and attractive, Sarah had suitors. None of them interested her, but one especially determined fellow in Limestone pursued her until she agreed to marry him "out of loneliness, not love." Loneliness would have been better. To rustle up cash, he pressed her into selling her house and buying a cheap trailer. He spent her money and abused her. The losses came so hard and so fast that she left him before their first anniversary.

In 1957, she hired on as a housekeeper for a divorced farmer with three children, who offered a home to her kids. Welcoming a new beginning, she pulled her boys out of the Indian boarding school. When neighbors began to talk about the arrangement, the farmer suggested they marry. "That," said Sarah, "was a marriage of convenience for both of us. We never even shared a bed." Within months of their wedding, he began drinking heavily. Nonetheless, weary and wary of repeated change, she stayed with him four years – until 1961 when their troubled nest resulted in one of her teenage boys landing in a detention home. Moving on yet again, Sarah found work and peaceful shelter caring for an elderly couple. She nursed them until they died. First one. . . and then the other.

By 1963, at age 36, Sarah had four failed marriages behind her and countless heartbreaks. She was at the end of her rope and hung there for quite some time. She, who had struggled through living with numerous alcoholics, all but gave up and turned to drinking herself. I've heard alcoholism described as a slow form of suicide, and in desolation Sarah joined that grave journey – to a point. "For nearly six years," she confessed, "I lived with Micmac friends and did almost nothing but drink and help them make baskets. Then I got fed up with myself. Sometimes you have to hit rock bottom before you can find the will to get up."

Once again, Sarah found refuge and purpose in caring for others, but this time the results were different. She took a job with a Maliseet Indian war veteran named

Perley, who hired her to look after his aging parents at the home he shared with them in Caribou, Maine. After they died in 1970, Sarah agreed to stay on to keep house for Perley, who was in his sixties and had become a friend. It was a crossroads moment. As she put it: "I was thinking, *by the old jibbers, I've got to buck up and turn my life around*!" She decided to get serious about basketry, a practiced skill rooted in her Micmac heritage: "I figured out how I could actually make a living weaving baskets. All I needed was someone to help – and then, all of sudden, out of nowhere, up shows Abe." She had never stopped loving the man behind the alcohol.

They started over. They found a house and moved in together. And they made beautiful baskets together. Both of them loved the work. Abe found and felled the ash trees and pounded the trunks into wood strips, which Sarah transformed into sturdy harvest baskets. Whenever she finished a potato basket, she threw it down hard, not to *test* its strength but to *prove* its strength – to demonstrate that she could make something that would not break.

"After a while," she recalled, "Perley missed company and my good cooking, so he moved in with us and we taught him a thing or two about baskets so he could help." Sometimes, said Sarah, but far less often than in the past, "Abe would go on a drunk." But he did not abuse her, he always came back, and Perley was on hand as balancer for both of them.

The only things more stunning to me than the repeated hardships Sarah faced were her resilience and the gratitude she expressed that the last chapter of her life was better than the beginning and the middle. In the 1980s, her daughter Mary came looking for her and Abe, expecting nothing from the parents who had abandoned her. A dozen years later, after Sarah's death, Mary wrote to me about that visit:

> *My mother had changed. She was so warm-hearted and being with her made me feel so good inside that I cried. She put her arms around me and said, 'I love you girl. I am so sorry. . . .' Each morning I watched birds flock to her for feeding, and at night we had long talks in her bedroom. Listening to her, I started to believe in angels. Saying goodnight, I would hug and kiss her on her cheek. . . . Before I left, she made me a basket while I watched, and she gave me a blanket that she made. I still have both, and sometimes I bring the blanket out to hug. To me, my mother had become a grand lady.*

What is the measure of a life? The breadth and depth of our troubles or the moments we transcend them with love? Our failings or our contributions? Looking at Sarah's life through a broad scope, distinct contributions come into view. For example, beyond all the people she took care of in her lifetime, she helped keep the declining traditional art of indigenous basketry alive. She did that by distributing her work through the Aroostook Band of Micmacs' Basket Bank, by teaching others how to weave, by participating in the documentary film *Our Lives in Our Hands,* which chronicled the lives of her people, and by making a basket for the band's permanent museum collection.

Moreover, Sarah shared her story. Her detailed descriptions of how she and Abe, as well as her parents and grandparents, followed seasonal work opportunities back-and-forth across the US-Canada border, provided evidence of Micmac presence in Maine through time. This was a vital piece in the tribe's federal recognition and land claim case, which came to a successful conclusion in 1991.

For me, professionally, piecing together the oral history of Sarah and other Micmacs had a significant influence on my work: It drove home the importance of aiming to write in a way that serves not only scholarship but is also meaningful to the people about whom one is writing. It set me on a course of working collaboratively. And it shed light on the power of biography to convey history in a compelling, empathetic and widely accessible way.

And for me personally, Sarah's story put my own challenges in perspective. It was not just the realization that my troubles paled dramatically in comparison to hers. It was how her story became an enduring call to never give up no matter what life throws at you and to find a way to make sure that the end is better than the beginning – even if your beginning was good. When I hit a rough patch and fall down, when I feel off center or unproductive, I hear Sarah saying, "By the old jibbers, I've got to buck up and turn my life around!" Her resilience is a spark for my fire. Her life is a reminder that it is never too late to find or rekindle your light.

EARTHSHINE

REALIZATION

The drum of the realization of the promise is beating.
~ Rumi

Sorrow has its reward.
It never leaves us where it found us.
~ Mary B. Eddy

One day in 1988, when I was about to board the plane that would take me back to Africa for a writing assignment, my husband embraced me and whispered in my ear, "Why are you always going so far away when there's so much to write about here?" Then he handed me a newspaper clipping about Molly Spotted Elk, a Penobscot Indian dancer from Maine, who lived from 1903-1977. The article featured a closeup photograph of her delicate face propped up on her hands and looking straight into the camera. I slipped the newsclip into my notebook and during the next two months abroad, I looked at it often. I found the picture enthralling and hauntingly ambiguous. Molly's dark eyes drew me in, but when I took a long deep look, they signaled "this far and no farther." I couldn't get her out of my mind. By the time I returned home to Maine, I knew I wanted to learn more about her – and perhaps write her story.

Since Molly was no longer living, I called her youngest sister, Dr. Eunice Bauman Nelson, an anthropologist my husband and I knew through our Native rights work with the Mi'kmaq. I told her I would like to talk with her about Molly and invited her to come for a visit. We spent a long weekend together, mostly sitting on our deck overlooking the Kennebec River and talking about four of Eunice's favorite topics: string theory, shamanism, nutrition and Molly. She credited Molly with teaching her so much about life – how to paddle a canoe, where to find wild berries, how to identify birds by their songs, the value of books and education, and the inexplicable power of dance and other arts to awaken the human spirit. Eunice recalled that the one time she saw Molly dance professionally, her own heart pounded and her body trembled. She encouraged me to go forward with the idea of writing about Molly and suggested I get in touch with Molly's daughter, Jean Moore – a psychic who at that time lived in Tennessee.

I wrote Jean, and within a week, she invited me to her home. For five days, we talked about her mother, breaking only for meals. My little recorder hummed morning till night as Jean reminisced and ruminated aloud about Molly's successes and struggles and how both had spilled over onto her. She sighed. She questioned. She laughed. She wept. By the end of our time together, I wept with her – about the depth of Molly's yearning to realize her place in the world, about the exquisite moments she found herself there, and about the times she lost her way, only to crawl back on bleeding knees. When it came time for me to go home, Jean entrusted me with boxes of her mother's memorabilia – correspondence, photographs, newsclips, promotional flyers, and personal diaries. Back home, I opened up those boxes, and they opened up a world to me.

At times it was heart-rending to read Molly's most intimate thoughts alongside newspaper articles written about her for public consumption. The first articulated what she longed and strived for in life and art. It captured the sweeping joys and sorrows of what it means to be human, especially what it meant to be a Native woman showcased in a non-Native world during the early decades of the 20th century. The second, mostly cliché entertainment news, suggested a wariness about revealing her private self and exposed the shallow questions and observations of journalists filtered through whatever prejudices they brought to a performance or interview. Even with the best reporters, Molly proved to be a *this-far-and-no-farther* subject. Yet, curiously, as I poured over her own words about her life, I had the sense that she penned her diaries not only for herself, but in the hope that one day, when she was no longer here and vulnerable, someone or some others would read what she wrote and understand the truth of her life.

Molly's diaries stretch from her teenage years through her forties. They chronicle her tireless and often encumbered efforts to preserve and foster respect for Native traditions through dance and writing. She performed mostly Indian dances for primarily white crowds, first in the United States, later in France. Unlike French audiences, she noted, Americans usually applauded "war whoops and savage gestures" over authenticity. Sometimes they taunted her. Other times, they romanticized and idealized her in ways she could never live up to.

Facing such reactions in her public and private life, Molly wrestled with a discrepancy between internal and external definitions of who she was. In one diary entry she lamented, "I'm just an injun in the flesh parade." In another she sighed, "There is no romantic appeal to the modern white in an eastern tribe of Indians. So, when they want a Sioux, oop, I'm one – the universal Indian." The knotted thread that ran through her life was an identity search – a quest to figure out what of her personal and indigenous past she could and would carry into her future, and a relentless effort to fit together the two worlds that tugged at her. Reading her diaries, I realized that the aim of those journals, at least in part, was to affirm her Penobscot self in the coercive arena of culture loss and assimilation.

Often, as I researched Molly's valiant struggle to free herself from the impositions of dominant society and its self-serving rendition of American history, I found myself reflecting on the ways that all of us, in measure, are shaped and shackled by our environment. Molly never surrendered the fight to carve a path through limitations imposed upon her by others, whether those constraints came from non-Natives or her own people. The conscious and deliberate choosing to be true to oneself while trying to move gracefully through an oft-contrary world is just one of many pieces of inspiration that came to me through this woman I never met yet grew to love and admire.

Molly's life began on Indian Island, the heart of the Penobscot Reservation in Old Town, Maine. The 375-acre island, shaped like an arrowhead, rises from the river that bears the name of her people. Her family's purse was small. Her father fished, hunted and kept a kitchen garden. Her mother made baskets to sell. Molly, the eldest of eight children, began performing professionally in her teens to help support the family. As she told her diary in her teenage years, "If I become a famous, Mama won't have to make baskets anymore."

With each passing year, talent, beauty, and determination afforded Molly a widening range of opportunities, from vaudeville and Wild West shows to chic New York nightclubs, to the lead female role in *The Silent Enemy* – a 1930 docudrama about Ojibwe Indians surviving a hunger winter in the remote forests of northern Ontario. Critics lauded the movie for its commitment to authenticity, evident in its all-Native cast, painstaking recreation of traditional Ojibwe material culture, and stunning cinematography of the natural world. Molly relished what she referred to as the "stupendous" endeavor of filming on location for a year in the Canadian wilderness. For her, it was the best of all worlds to collaborate with sophisticated filmmakers while living in a tent, paddling a canoe, and spending time with what she referred to as "bush Indians," who were still intimately connected to every howl, whisper and whoosh in their natural habitat.

In 1931, Molly danced before European royalty and heads of state in an opening act for the Colonial Exposition in Paris. This extravaganza flaunted the resources and diverse cultures of colonized countries, while idealizing the "civilizing" influences of France and other colonial powers. Molly and the U.S. Indian Band headlined the United States display, performing daily at a replica of George Washington's Mount Vernon estate. She also performed at nightclubs and other venues around the city and wrote the only known indigenous account of the exposition, which attracted some 33 million visitors during the six months it was open.

When the exposition closed, Molly remained in France, drawn by European audiences, which seemed more appreciative than Americans of the authentic traditional dances she cherished. She moved in with Jean Archambaud, a *Paris Soir* journalist with whom she'd fallen into a passionate love affair after he interviewed her for the paper. Opportunities to perform in Paris and other venues across France grew, and occasionally Jean appeared on stage with her, drumming while she danced. When she was asked to advise on a North American Indian exhibition at the Trocadéro Ethnographic Museum, he wrote about it. Sometimes, they coauthored articles, and he steadfastly encouraged her to complete a book of the Penobscot legends that tribal elders had shared with her in exchange for chores when she was a girl. Beyond writing for newspapers and magazines, Jean penned a stream of love letters to Molly, often waxing romantic about their shared love for nature, realized in numerous hiking and camping adventures noted in her diaries. While living in the City of Lights, Molly found her inner light and a work-love balance that took her by surprise, for earlier she had told her diary, "Sooner or later, I, as a woman, will have to make a choice between two things: I will be happy in my work and lonely, or happy with someone and discontented with myself and my work."

In 1934, Jean and Molly had a child together and named her after him. Four years later, they married – only to be ripped apart by WWII. When German troops marched into France in 1940, Jean went into hiding, and Molly fled on foot with their little daughter across the Pyrenees Mountains into Spain. Ultimately, mother and child made it home to the Penobscot reservation, and Jean found safety in a refugee center in southern France. In the ensuing months, Molly and Jean wrote to one another almost daily, numbering the envelopes in order to track whether their letters made it through the vicissitudes of wartime mail service.

One day, an unnumbered envelope arrived from the refugee center written in a hand Molly didn't recognize. Cautiously, she opened it and unfolded its contents. The letter began: "The present war caused many sorrowful losses…" It ended: "He died with your name on his lips."

It was a message impossible to absorb. Shock turned into a sorrow so massive that it pressed Molly into the depths of depression and eventually into a mental institution. There, turning to her diary for solace, she strove to make sense of her life through writing, reflecting on her situation with an astuteness that would have surprised her doctors. After a year, they released her into the care of her mother, who lived in the comfortable house Molly had bought for the family with her earnings from *The Silent Enemy.*

Sheltered in the home she'd gifted to others, Molly spent the latter years of her life on Indian Island – reading, writing, making Indian dolls, walking the forest, and sitting by the Penobscot River, watching its flow come and go all at once. Her daughter Jean had married and moved away, but when she visited with her children, Molly took them on woodland adventures. She told them legends and showed them how to catch a fish by hand. Occasionally, young Penobscots came by to ask her about old traditions, and teachers at the reservation school invited her to talk to their classes and teach them tribal dances. Life had become quiet and contained compared to her years in New York and Paris. But there was relief in its simplicity. And contentment. And even joy.

Initially, as a non-Native, I wrestled with my role as Molly's biographer. I'll never forget the first time I saw a pair of her size 5 dance moccasins. Looking from them to my size 9 feet, I thought, *I'll never be able to step into her shoes and tell her story.*

Yet, the coming together of contrasting lives from distinct cultures was both the process and the purpose of Molly's biography. And, as I discovered while researching and writing, Molly held this as a central purpose in her life. She endeavored to build a bridge between Penobscot culture and the larger world in which she moved. The first stage name she chose for herself was *Neeburban*, the Penobscot word for Northern Lights. In many ways, this name symbolizes the light or insight Molly sought for herself and shared with others through her art. She once told her diary, "With patience and hard work, I will reach that hilltop I want to reach so badly – not fame, but realization."

Reading her words, I recognized a shared desire. I, too, yearned for realization. I wanted to understand the inner and outer forces that shape a life – my own, as well as those that appear to be so different from mine. I wanted to write a book that pressed me and readers to reach across cultural divides as Molly did. It seemed to me that if I grew to know her and then introduced her to others in a way that prompted them to take her arm and walk open-heartedly through her life, we would become co-witnesses to particular adversities and strengths that would shatter deep-seated stereotypes, stir empathy, and help pry open channels of communication. I harbored the hope that if we understood one another more we would damage each other less.

Ultimately, among the contrasts in our lives, I found many commonalities – shared ground where I could stand beside Molly and make sense of our differences. These ranged from our cross-cultural marriages to a deep love for nature and a desire to do purposeful work. Concerning work, her life taught me that the fruits of one's labor may take a long time to ripen.

Molly died in 1977, living just long enough to see the dawn of Penobscot cultural renewal. Year by year, recognition of her contribution to that Native renaissance grows. Beyond the way she chose to live her life, which reveals the possibilities of cherishing tradition while embracing a wider world, the film she starred in – *The Silent Enemy* – has been reissued as a classic. Two of the Indian dolls she made are now in the Smithsonian, and the diaries and other memorabilia recording her tragedies and triumphs are preserved in the Special Collections archives at University of Maine, Orono, just downriver from the reservation. The publishing of her book of legends, interrupted by WWII, finally came to fruition 25 years after her passing. Artists and academics have turned her story into songs, beadwork, stage performances, and scholarly articles. And in 2023, a half-page belated obituary about her appeared in *The New York Times*. All of these are cultural anchors and springboards for new generations of Penobscots. They prove true something Molly foretold in her diary: "The beautiful things live on to heal the wounds of sorrow."

I hold to that thought. It has lifted me up countless times.

ONE SMALL LAMP

The waning moon still has not risen.
Our one small lamp struggles against the wind. ~ Li Po

Our greatest glory is not in never falling,
but in rising every time we fall. ~ Confucius

In the spring of 1978, I traveled to mainland China to chronicle the aftermath of its Cultural Revolution, the communist regime's ruthless movement that wrecked and ended countless lives and also ransacked and destroyed historical, cultural and religious sites. During the month-long sojourn, I spent several days in Beijing. As my translator and I drove to the hotel – the only one in the city available to foreigners at that time – I was struck by the scarcity of cars and the massive traffic jams of bikes. It did not look or feel like the capital of a global superpower, as it does today.

One afternoon, I noticed most of the hotel staff streaming through a door near the reception desk. When the flow stopped, the door remained open. Peeking in, I saw some two-dozen people crammed into a room, their eyes fixed on a small black-and-white television. Noticing my curiosity, a fellow standing by the door whispered, "English lessons." He stepped aside to let me in. Soon, my eyes were also riveted to the teacher on the TV screen – a petite woman dressed in a loose Mao jacket and trousers, like nearly everyone in China at the time. Her magnetic presence defied that prescribed garb. She taught with gusto, enunciating words with demanding precision, inviting her audience to repeat after her, and then flashing an encouraging smile. Her persona seemed to hold promise for a positive new chapter in the People's Republic of China.

Twenty-five years later, I flew to Geneva, Switzerland, for my first meeting as a board member of an international women's organization. The other members hailed from Canada, India, Sierra Leone, Switzerland and China. At dinner after our first day together, I sat next to the vice chair, Wu Qing, who had an aura of purposeful confidence infused with irresistible warmth. Hearing that she had been an English professor in Beijing, I asked, on a whim, "Are you by chance the woman I saw teaching on Chinese television in 1978?"

"You were in China then?!" she exclaimed.

When I nodded, she squared her shoulders and responded with obvious pride, "Yes, that was me. I taught the country English."

After that encounter, Wu Qing and I saw each other regularly at board meetings in Geneva or New

York. When apart, we stayed in touch through email and occasionally by phone. As time passed, our friendship grew, and I learned more about her. I learned that she'd been born in the storm of war, navigated political blizzards and confronted totalitarian tempests without losing her faith in humankind nor her determination to call forth the best of what it means to be human.

Wu Qing's life began in 1937 in the arms of remarkable parents who, as she likes to say, met "on a slow boat to America" in 1923. Her mother, age 23, was on her way to Wellesley College, where she would earn a master's degree in American Literature and develop a keen interest in written works created within and beyond the borders of the United States. Her father, age 22, was heading to Dartmouth College before going on to Columbia University, where he did coursework in anthropology and sociology and earned a PhD in the latter.

After studying and traveling abroad, Wu Qing's father, Wu Wenzao, founded sociology and cultural anthropology programs at Beijing's Yenching University, noted for having strong ties with Western scholars. Her mother, Xie Wanying, already an established writer known by her pen name Bing Xin ("Heart Pure as Ice") also taught there. During her undergraduate years at Yenching, she had published lyrical poems and short stories about childhood and nature, as well as a much-read essay inspired by her involvement in the 1919 May Fourth Movement – a patriotic student uprising, which she described as a "thunderous and determined struggle against imperialism and feudalism." In the years that followed, Bing Xin became one of China's most revered and prolific 20th-century authors and a translator of esteemed literary works, including Bengali-Indian poet Rabindranath Tagore's *The Gardener* and Lebanese-American poet Khalil Gibran's *The Prophet*. Her translations worked in subtle ways to foreground women and obscure social rank and gender identity. In her own writing, she broke new ground as a literary modernist driven by a philosophy of universal love. Her life motto was simply: "With love, everything is possible."

After Bing Xin and Wu Wenzao married in 1929, her love credo was put to test repeatedly over decades of violent upheavals in China. First, they lived through eight years of terror and turmoil during the Chinese War of Resistance Against Japan. It began in the summer of 1937, when Bing Xin was pregnant with Wu Qing, the last of their three children. Eight months after her birth, the family fled 1600 miles southwest to the city of Kunming in Yunnan Province. There, like millions of others escaping to parts of the country not occupied by

Japan, they began reassembling their lives under the war's long dark shadow. Wu Qing's father established a sociology department at a new war-time university. He called upon other refugee scholars to join him in studying dozens of minority ethnic groups in Han-dominant mainland China. As he saw it, the program matched his conviction that knowledge about different ways of being and thinking would make it possible for the country he loved to establish equity and unity in diversity.

In 1940, when Japan joined Nazi Germany and the other Axis powers, China's War of Resistance Against Japan became part of WWII. By then, the Republic of China's central government, controlled by the Nationalist Party, had retreated to Chongqing in Sichuan Province. Wu Qing's family moved there, her father to assume a government liaison position while continuing his research, her mother to serve as an elected deputy in the Nationalist Congress. As China's temporary capital, Chongqing formed the nation's political, military, diplomatic and cultural nucleus for nearly a decade, and from 1942-45, it served as the regional command center of the Allied powers.

In Chongqing, as in Kunming, Wu Qing's parents met and interacted with a global array of scholars, politicians, diplomats, foreign advisors and military officers. Beyond public service, Bing Xin continued her writing. Most notably, she researched and wrote, *About Women*, a group portrait of 14 female Chinese intellectuals of the day. Ingeniously, she published this feminist tome under the pen name "Mr. Man." Like everyone else's work, hers was done in fits and starts between air raids.

As for Wu Qing, who grew from infancy to girlhood during this war-torn time, when I asked her about her earliest memory, she described playing in the woods near their home on the outskirts of Kunming and Chongqing: "My nanny had bound feet, so she couldn't go out, but from the time I could walk, my parents had taught me to be responsible for myself. So, I was allowed to explore the forest on my own even though I was so young. I had a lot of time and space to learn about nature – and about courage. There were air raids almost daily, and I learned to hurry to the caves to escape Japanese bombers. The shelters were cold, dark, and crowded."

When, at last, the war ended in 1945, the United States led the Allied powers in the occupation and rehabilitation of Japan. Wu Qing's father accepted a diplomatic post in Tokyo. Once there, he taught at Tokyo University, in addition to playing a lead role in the Chinese Mission working with Americans on military, political, economic and social reforms – and helping pave the way for the Republic of China to become a founding member of the United Nations. Bing Xin immersed herself in the new setting, teaching Chinese Literature at the university, cultivating relationships with Japanese women, and penning essays encouraging mothers around the world to contribute to global peace by forging cross-cultural friendships.

While her parents focused on finding ways to mend the wounds of war and reposition China's place in the world, 9-year-old Wu Qing rebelled against having to live with the former enemy. She organized a gang with the kids of other foreign diplomats and staff, and they ventured out on their bikes to chase down and scare Japanese children. When her mother heard about it, she sat Wu Qing down for a stern talk: *How could you do that? You are spreading seeds of hatred. What have those children done to you? Some of their parents were killed or imprisoned because they protested the war!*

Wu Qing remembers that childhood scolding as a turning point for her – the moment when she first learned to distinguish between people and the governmental structures that shape our lives in so many ways. She says it was also the moment when she began to glean what it meant to be a true human being and a global citizen. Her mother's lessons about widening the borders of one's life were reinforced at the English-speaking International School of the Sacred Heart, which Wu Qing attended during their years in Tokyo. "I changed," Wu Qing says. " I made friends with my Japanese neighbors. I learned the importance of loving people throughout the world." She describes the years in Tokyo as "American in lifestyle. We bought things from the [U.S. Army] PX, we watched American films, listened to American broadcasts, and read *The Stars & Stripes*, the U.S. military newspaper.

Meanwhile, China's civil war between its US-aided Nationalist Party and Soviet-backed Communist Party, which had been largely suspended in order to defeat their common enemy, had reignited in 1945. In 1949, it culminated in a communist victory and the founding of the People's Republic of China (PRC), with Mao Zedong at the helm as the all-powerful chairman of the Chinese Communist Party. Defeated, the Nationalist government and some one million loyalists (about half of them military) retreated to China's island of Taiwan, turning that province into a separate republic. This split into two Chinas forced Wu Qing's parents into a radical decision about the future of their family. Their dilemma was difficult and too complex for their twelve-year-old daughter to fully comprehend, but one major factor was the outbreak of a war between recently partitioned North and South Korea. Within months, the Korean War

EARTHSHINE

escalated into an international conflict that unraveled U.S.-China relations. American troops based in Japan were deployed to support the regime in South Korea, while the new PRC sent hundreds of thousands of soldiers into communist North Korea in support of their ideological allies seeking to restore the peninsula as a unified state. As the ground beneath their feet shifted, creating confusion and pitfalls in every direction, Bing Xin and Wu Wenzao made a risky choice to return to the city where they'd both come of age on mainland China.

Starting anew in Beijing, they joined the China Association for Promoting Democracy – one in a handful of non-communist parties. Both hoped there was still space for them to play a role in creating a country that nurtured the contributions and wellbeing of its entire diverse population. Wu Qing recalls how tricky it was for them to get situated in the PRC. "Right after we returned my parents were required to write formal statements about their relationship with the Nationalist government because the Communist Party was suspicious of them." Nearly two years passed before both of them were professionally reestablished – Wu Wenzao as director of ethnology (cultural anthropology) programs at Minzu University and Bing Xin as a key member in the government-sanctioned China Writers Association and, beginning in 1954, as an elected deputy in the newly formed National People's Congress. As it turned out, the political party they joined was powerless – a fact that remains true to this day for all of the country's non-communist parties, which collectively account for less than 15 percent of the congressional body. "My daddy had a vision of what China could be," says Wu Qing, "but in the end, he was cheated. Many people were cheated by Mao, who said China would be a country of freedom and opportunity for everyone with all the parties working together. That did not happen."

Life in new China came nowhere near the idealistic hopes Wu Qing's parents held for themselves, their children and their country. As Western-educated intellectuals who did not join the Communist Party, they experienced new kinds of instability and suffering under Mao's continuous agitation against the country's "bourgeoisie" class – intellectuals, diplomats, prominent businessmen and noted artists.

In 1957, after a year-long campaign inviting differing views concerning national policy, the Party cracked down on those who took up the offer. That included Wu Wenzao, who was labeled as a "rightist"[2] and banned from the university for the ideas he put forth,

---

[2] The term "rightist" referred to intellectuals who appeared to favor capitalism against collectivization.

such as challenging one-party rule, teaching the principle of "unity amidst diversity" and urging China to remain neutral in the Cold War between the United States and Russia and their respective allies. As for Bing Xin, with publishing increasingly controlled by the Communist Party, it became impossible to weave political reflections into her writing as she'd done previously. With an eye toward survival, she focused on nonpolitical writing, maintaining her literary position and her message of love. The Party welcomed her stories about family and motherhood, especially multiple editions of her *Letters to Young Readers*, which they endorsed as pedagogical tools to promote patriotism as a natural and unconditional emotion echoing the love children have for their mothers. Bing Xin didn't buy the comparison. When pressed to condemn her husband and praise the Party, she refused, but that small act of resistance did not ease her soul.

Meanwhile, Wu Qing focused on her high school studies at #13 Girls School in Beijing. Upon graduation in 1957, she feared she'd be blocked from higher education because her father had been condemned. "But then," she recalls, "Beijing Foreign Language University accepted me because I had a background in English and new China needed lots of interpreters." Politics infused every aspect of her university years: "There was one political movement after another, and we did more physical labor than studies. I spent most of my time working in a tile factory managing 70 other English students. Mao pushed the idea that the more knowledge you have the more 'reactionary' you are. Critical thinking was his enemy. He said 5 percent of all people ought to be labeled as 'rightists' and instructed students to look for them among their peers and report them to government officials."

In 1959, when China's close political relationship with the Soviet Union was deteriorating over ideological quarrels about Marxist-Leninist doctrine, students at Beijing's Foreign Studies University who had been preparing for further education and work in Russia, lined up to get into the English Department instead. "Because of that and the high marks I had on my exams," Wu Qing recalls, "I was given the opportunity to become a teacher. My mom said, 'That's wonderful, you'll be close to home.' My daddy said, 'You're not yet qualified!' But once I became a teacher, I prepared seriously for every class and became a favorite among students."

A certain young professor also favored Wu Qing. "In 1962, my best friend told me that my colleague Chen Su, who taught English literature, would like to court me. I hadn't been interested in men, but I had known him since I'd come to the university as a student. I knew he was kind, down to earth, hardworking and responsible. So I said, 'Ok, he can try.' Two years later we got married. And the next year, we had our son. We were given a dorm room in the school."

During the first half of the 1960s, life was relatively sweet for Wu Qing's new little family and her parents. Wu Wenzao was fully reinstated at Minzu University and reclaimed his role as a highly esteemed professor and leader in his field. Although Bing Xin's writing repertoire was still curtailed, she remained prolific and also continued translating notable works by others. But then came another political storm, far worse than the 1957 crackdown.

In 1966, the year Wu Qing turned 29, Mao launched the Cultural Revolution, a brutal campaign to purge any remnants of the traditional upper class and modern capitalist elements from Chinese society. Traditional elites, branded as "bourgeoisie," were ripped from their jobs, publicly humiliated, and banished to rural areas for hard labor. Wu Qing, her husband and her parents all faced public "struggling" sessions – verbal and physical abuse orchestrated by the Communist Party. One day, paramilitary Red Guards burst into her parents' home, dragged them outside and made them kneel on rough ground for hours while they ransacked the place and hauled away family heirlooms and other treasured objects. Acting as Mao's minions, these militant student gangs took those treasures, along with valuable items plucked from other prominent citizens, to Wu Wenzao's university for display in a single public-shaming exhibition titled, "The Bourgeois Life of Wu Wenzao and Bing Xin." For ten days, the elderly couple had to stand at the entryway with their shoes on their ears and blackboards hanging from their necks proclaiming their guilt as "class enemies."

Worst of all for Wu Qing were struggling sessions that included interrogations about colleagues. During one of our phone visits, she described how Red Guards kept pressing her to incriminate the school's president as someone who had supported students protesting the violent suppression. "Repeatedly, I told them that the president could not have been involved due to illness. Then they started to threaten my son at his nursery school." As she relived this story, her pace quickened, and her words spilled out like gravel. "He was only two years old and came home on the weekends. . . . He started having nightmares." Here Wu Qing choked up and her gravelly words now came out in fits and starts. "I was afraid they wouldn't let him come home – I gave up – I told a lie – It was only when I said what they wanted to hear that they stopped threatening my son . . . ." At this point, I could tell she was speaking through tears. "I had *never* lied. My parents forbade it. I felt *awful*. I said to myself I would *never* again let that happen."

All told, Wu Qing suffered close to 80 struggling sessions at her university. After one session of merciless taunts and insults by dozens of combative students, a few dared to approach her in secret to say, "We're sorry professor; we were forced to do that." But their clandestine apologies did nothing to keep her and her loved ones from deportation to large collective farms as forced laborers: "When all the struggling meetings in Beijing were over, my parents and I were sent to rural areas to do grueling physical labor and participate in training to change our thinking. I was forced to carry huge bundles of harvested rice all day long in temperatures that hung around 90 degrees. I had to do it *running*. If I didn't go fast enough, they would hold struggle meetings against me, and I'd have to bend my head and take the abuse." During Wu Qing's banishment, her husband Chen Su remained in Beijing and took care of their son. "Chen Su was a very quiet person," she told me, "reserved, not outspoken, not challenging. He didn't say yes or no – or *lie*."

After a year of rural exile, Wu Qing's parents were allowed to return to Beijing, in part because they were needed to translate Richard Nixon's book, *Six Crises*, which he had written in the hope of gaining political traction after losing his first presidential bid to John F. Kennedy. Authorities also let Wu Qing go home because one side of her body had gone numb, and she needed emergency medical attention. But for the duration of the devastating decade-long purge, Wu Wenzao was barred from his professorship. For a long stretch of time, he was required to do physical labor on the campus and often wasn't permitted to go home at night. He and other professors slept on mats in one room. Sometimes, members of the Red Guard would burst into the dorm, wake him up, beat him and denounce him, declaring, "Even in your dreams you're talking like a reactionary!"

Bing Xin suffered equally. For three-and-a-half years, officials required her to travel five hours round trip to clean toilets at the China Writers Association – an organization for which she had played an important leadership role since its founding in 1949. As for Wu Qing, in 1971, amid the ongoing cruelties of the Cultural Revolution, she was given the opportunity to return to her university post because Communist China was about to replace Taiwan as a member of the United Nations, which made foreign language training important again.

Mao's death in 1976 signaled the end of the revolution's draconian regime. Two years later – the same year I saw Wu Qing teaching English on Chinese television – the National People's Congress enacted a new constitution. It enshrined "four big rights," all centered on free speech. Under China's new supreme leader, Deng Xiaoping, Wu Wenzao was finally, yet again, allowed to return to his university position. This latest shift gave him a glimmer of hope, but it was short lived. Within a few years, alarmed by escalating public criticism, Congress revoked the four big rights, and he felt gagged once more. Wu Qing, however, took the backtracking as a call to action. "The more my family and I got knocked down," she told me, "the more I wanted to change things, so others won't have to go through what we did."

Despite that setback, efforts to bring about change gained wider berth under Deng, who called for "courageous experiments" to transform China's economy and build a modern infrastructure at record speed. He also created some space for new cultural expressions and the emergence of nongovernmental organizations.

In 1984, at age 47, Wu Qing won an elected seat in the People's Congress of Beijing's Haidian District, home to some 3 million people and more than a dozen universities. The next year she established the Women Studies Forum, one of China's first nongovernmental organizations. Traveling widely to promote gender awareness and women's empowerment, she took time to listen to the stories of poor people in remote areas. The plight of rural women appalled her – their high rate of illiteracy and the fact that they contributed two-thirds of the country's labor and were commonly pressed into arranged marriages that resembled enslavement. Determined to help improve their lives, she founded a training center in the outskirts of Beijing where young rural women can come to widen their skillsets and learn about entrepreneurship, political action and economic independence. She also initiated China's first university course on feminism and began speaking widely within and beyond China on women's issues. Turn by turn, she unscrewed the lid from her mother's political inkwell and wrote her own activist's story.

Developing a vision of what she could achieve for her constituents, Wu Qing did a deep dive into the PRC's constitution, significantly revised in 1982. She combed over it, highlighting every item that had anything to do with civil rights. Paying keen attention to language and detail, she came to the conclusion that it provided more political and social space than most people realized. Most notably, in her eyes, it included an explicit mandate for congressional deputies like herself to supervise the work of the central government officials. She began asserting herself, insisting that China's laws be honored and not casually overridden by authorities. By 1988, she had hit her stride and gained a seat in the larger Beijing Municipal People's Congress. The year she assumed that office, she cast her first "no" vote – a rare expression of public disapproval of Party policy. "I became a thorn in the sides of many government officials," she told me with a laugh and an air of *this is what it takes.* She had found her voice and would not be intimidated into silence.

The mission Wu Qing set for herself is as clear as it is challenging: "I want to change the system from one governed by rule of man to one governed by rule of law." Toward that end, she made a habit to carry copies of the constitution with her and hand them out to her constituents. When they voiced a complaint, she would tell them, "Read the constitution to see what your rights are in this area and then we'll work on it." She took the unprecedented step of opening her office one day a week to meet directly with the people she represented. "Listening," she says, "is fundamental to democracy. You must listen with 15 hearts – especially to those who have different views." This is her mantra.

Wu Qing's open mind and fearless frankness have not sat well with authorities. In 1989, the year she stood in support of student-led anti-government demonstrations in Beijing's Tiananmen Square, the Communist Party branch at her university announced that she would not be permitted to stand for re-election to the Haidian District People's Congress. Voters defied the authoritarian ruling and elected her, nonetheless, citing a bureaucratic statute that said anyone who received ten nominations could run for office. She won by a landslide. Some years later, after returning home from a conference in Norway where she spoke on the dire status of human rights in China, she wasn't allowed to leave her country for three years. In the year 2000, her relentless principled stance led to forced early retirement from her professorship.

All told, Wu Qing served 27 years in the Haidian District People's Congress (1984-2011) and 19 years in the Beijing Municipal People's Congress (1988-2007). To this day, she remains devoted to her mission, working across many fronts to take a stand for women, the rule of law, and human rights. She serves on the boards of several non-governmental organizations and remains deeply involved with the Practical Skills Training Center for Rural Women she founded 25 years ago. When new students arrive there, they are greeted by a plaque at the entrance inscribed with her mother's famous motto, "With love, everything is possible." Wu Qing makes a point of being on hand to welcome them and give an inspirational speech. She always mentions the function of the constitution, encourages students to stand as candidates in village elections, and puts forth her charge that it's their job as citizens to watch their government closely and use the law as a tool to prevent abuse of power.

Asked about the source of her courage, Wu Qing tells me that her confidence comes from the constitution and the people who rely upon her and support her. Beyond that, she feels protected by the eminence of her parents, especially her mother, whose *For Young Readers* stories continue to reach millions of Chinese students in their formative years. "Some people," she says, "use their famous parents to make money. I use mine to take a stand for human rights in general and women's rights in particular." Her sense of security is also shored up by international recognition for her own pathbreaking advocacy on behalf of women and the rule of law in China, including the 2001 Ramon Magsaysay Award (known as "Asia's Nobel Prize"). But most of all, it seems to me, her bravery is fueled by a profound commitment to live up to the ideal of what it means to be human in the way she learned from her mother. That is the small, but brilliant lamp that lights her way as she presses forward through the dark clouds of political storms. It has become a lamp for me, as well.

One day years ago, when we were sitting in one of Geneva's many cafés, Wu Qing commented, "My mother taught me to be a rational, honest and loving person. In other words, she taught me what it means to be human." To illustrate the essence of that lesson, she reached for my notebook and pen and wrote down the Chinese character for human: 人 Then, undeterred by any onlookers, she stood up and assumed the pose of the two-legged character. "This," she said, "is *rèn* – a person, a human being. It's like a figure standing on two feet with the head tilting slightly to the left because that's where your heart is, and you have to listen to your heart." Then, elaborating on this personal interpretation of the symbol, she added: "I think one leg represents integrity and responsibility; the other learning and growing. That's what it means to be truly human."

As a language professor, Wu Qing relishes breaking down words, looking at their roots to find nuances of meaning. After expounding on the word "human," she offered her take on the Chinese character for harmony: "One part of the character means 'speak' and the other means 'everyone.' This implies that when everyone has the right to speak there will be harmony."

And then she turned to the word "listening," pointing out that it's comprised of several characters, including love, ear, eyes and virtue. As she spoke, her mantra about listening with 15 hearts came alive, and my sense of what that means swelled.

Sometimes, a friend or family member – or a stranger who happens to sit next to you on a plane – just needs a sounding board to bounce their thoughts against so they can discern them more clearly. Then, simply being empathetic and attentive is enough. Wu Qing does that. But most often, she is in 15-hearts attention mode – listening purposefully with an ear tuned toward thoughtful action that effects positive change. For her, listening and action are two sides of the same coin. "I am a verb," she proclaims. "I want to help turn China into a country that engenders freedom, democracy and rule of law. That requires action and it may take centuries to be realized. But nothing will change if we just sit here and complain. So, I am a verb, an active verb doing my bit to fulfill my responsibility as a human being."

At this writing, Wu Qing is 87 and has lived alone since the death of her beloved husband Chen Su in 2017. During one of our phone conversations this past summer, she told me, "I am alone, but not lonely." She had just completed biographies on her parents and was sensing their presence deeply, even though both died decades ago. She feels an urgency to pass on to the next generation what she learned from them, "not just skills and knowledge," she says, "but love, integrity and responsibility." The promise of an open China that shone through her face and voice when I saw her teaching English on television 45 years ago has fallen to pieces under the current regime with Xi Jinping as the paramount leader. But her vision and determination remain unbroken and her lamp undimmed. With the recent lifting of her country's severe Covid pandemic restrictions, she was once again able to travel and had recently returned from giving a talk in Geneva. Bold as ever, she asserted, "Chinese leaders are afraid of me because I speak the truth and talk about human rights. It's especially hard to do that now because things have gotten worse. China is being ruled by totalitarianism. You can be silent about that, but once you decide to speak, you have to tell the truth. Some young people are protesting and speaking out. Others want to. They come to me to talk. I listen. And so do they."

*

Postscript: Given the complexity of Wu Qing's story, once I was done, I asked her to read it for fact-checking purposes. Her feedback surprised me. She had only a few minor corrections, but one big disappointment: "Why did you not tell about my first dog? My experience with him explains why I am the way I am." I knew the story. She had told it to me several times, but I'd received it as a sweet childhood memory rather than a revelation about how her profound sense of responsibility toward others came into being. So here it is: "When I was about two-and-a-half years old, I was very fond of our neighbor's little dog, and I asked my mom if I could have a dog of my own. She had me sit down and gave me a very serious answer: "To have a dog, you have to do four things. Number 1, people eat and dogs eat, so you have to feed the dog. Number 2, people need to drink water every day, and so do dogs, so you have to give water to the dog daily. Number 3, there's not enough water to bathe the dog regularly, so you have to brush him clean. Number 4, in the forest where you play, there are wolves that could kill the dog if he's left out at night, so you need to bring him in before dusk. If you can do all those things, you may have a dog. Think it over." Even though I was so young, I was a thinking human being. I thought it over, and then I told my mother, 'Yes, I can do all those things.' And I did. It was a responsibility, a commitment, a trust. And it was love. These things have stayed with me all my life. That's why I think it's so important to include the story of my first dog."

ABOUT THE AUTHOR

Bunny McBride, journalist/author/anthropologist, has written numerous books on topics ranging from Native American biography to wildlife conservation to contemplative essays and poetry. Among those books are *Women of the Dawn, By the Light of the Moon,* and *The National Audubon Field Guide to African Wildlife.*

Made in United States
Troutdale, OR
11/29/2023

15106495R00092